MW01534850

DISCARDED

Legal Almanac Series No. 58

DICTIONARY OF SELECTED LEGAL TERMS AND MAXIMS

by
EDWARD J. BANDER, L.L.B.

*This legal almanac has been revised
by the Oceana Editorial Staff*

Irving J. Sloan
General Editor

SECOND EDITION

1979 Oceana Publications, Inc.
Dobbs Ferry, New York

Library of Congress Cataloging in Publication Data

Bander, Edward J.
    Dictionary of selected legal terms and maxims.

    (Legal almanac series ; no. 58)
    First ed. published in 1966 under title: Law
dictionary of practical definitions.

    1. Law—United States—Terms and phrases.
I. Sloan, Irving J.   II. Oceana Publications, Inc.
III. Title.
KF156.B36   1979   340'.03   79-19266
ISBN 0-379-11119-5

Manufactured in the United States of America

TABLE OF CONTENTS

INTRODUCTION

THE PERILS OF USING A LAW DICTIONARY

There is no mystery to law. A law dictionary such as this, which does not hesitate to quote Justices Holmes and Cardozo, which cites the reader to leading treatises such as Wigmore on *Evidence,* the *Restatements* and Corbin on *Contracts,* and which refrains from the standard law dictionary practice of wearying definitions that add to one's confusion, can easily instill the suspicion in a diligent patron of the law that he has the makings of an advocate.

In fact, every losing litigant is sure he could have handled his case better than counsel; doctors, dentists and optometrists are notorious for their belief that their profession's gain is the law's loss; and the jails are full of people who grudgingly admire only one sklil in lawyers, and that is counsel's ability to collect a sizable retainer before trial.

To these and others this law dictionary can be a vital tool. With it I offer, at the reluctance of my publisher, and with grave misgivings of censure from those who would keep the practice of law a mystery, a *vade mecum,* an open sesame, a law in a nutshell course that will painlessly lead one and all through the labyrinth of the law to the end result of justice, which to most means victory.

The first significant concept in finding the law is precedent (See DICTUM and OPINION in this dictionary). Simply stated this means that you must find a case in your JURISDICTION having the same basic pattern as your problem. If you find such a case, and it rests on all fours (as the lawyers say) as does your problem, your search is over. One or two technicalities must be observed; for instance, making sure the case is not decided against you on all fours. Should this occur, you have the option of convincing the court that it had erred in its previous reasoning. However, as this discussion is confined to law and not art, it is beyond the pale of this article.

Now, assuming a legal problem, how do we find the vital case that will decide it? I should say cases, because lawyers are usually dealing with a combination of cases, dexterously woven together into what is called a brief, and this word is indeed, a misnomer. The process is descriptively very simple. Two publishing houses do all the work for you. The first, in order of size, is the West Publishing Company, which offers to lawyers what they call a "Key" system. They publish the National Reporter System which carries the full text of all the high court cases in all the fifty states. Above each case are headnotes broken down into legal subject matters. The headnotes, from all these cases, are organized into *Digests*.

The granddaddy of all the digests is the American Digest System, which is arranged alphabetically from "Abandonment" to "Zoning"; and broken down within each subject matter so finely that you would think it was done by a blender instead of a host of near-sighted law editors.

If your problem is one in CONTRACT and involves "consideration," you simply open the digest to the volume containing "Contracts," run your finger down the yellowed pages until you get to "consideration." Here you will find a key number which, a few pages away, will lead you to a "myriad of precedents," as non-lawyer

Tennyson once wrote. You check the capsule description of cases, note the ones that deserve your attention, and you are in business.

Another method of research with the digests assumes utter ignorance of the law. For example, your child is injured by a baseball at a summer camp, simply look up "baseball" in the Fifth Decennial Digest *Descriptive Word Index* and you will find a page of situations involving baseballs that have caused legal disputes. Check the appropriate key numbers, take down citations to pertinent cases, read those cases and you have a familiarity with the law, which, you should be forewarned, could breed contempt of court.

To add to the simplicity, West has a third method—the "tip" approach. Somebody, be careful it is not a spy for your adversary, tips you off on a "case in point." This is even better than one on all fours. Locate this case in the Digest *Table of Cases* and you will not only find out the citation to the case but the key numbers it covers. And those key numbers can be music to your ears.

A few caveats or cautions, for those who prefer the vernacular, are now in order. The law, it must be stressed, is played by year. The more recent the ruling of a court, the better your chance of a favorable decision, unless the old decision was written by Lemuel Shaw or Justice Holmes or, possibly, William Blackstone, if you have a crusty old judge whose learning is such that he took law books with him on his honeymoon. Also, you must read the actual opinion of the court. Citing a headnote or digested item to a judge is like waving a red flag in front of a bull; and, to prolong the metaphor, why unnecessarily skewer yourself on the horns of a dilemma?

Publisher Number Two, the Lawyers Cooperative

Publishing Company, claims, like Avis, that although it is not so big as West, it is more diligent. They do not publish all the high court cases as does West, but only leading cases, and as an extra, offer exhaustive annotations on the legal matter discussed in the printed case. The case may have occurred in West Virginia, but the annotation will tell you how all the other states that have had a similar type of case decided it. If you can find a case in point in the *American Law Reports* of this publisher, a vast amount of looking up the law and the writing of a brief to present to the court has been accomplished. Those with the dubious good fortune to have read Travers, *Antomy of a Murder,* will soon realize that the only love scene in the book is when the protagonist's eyes fall on an *American Law Report* annotation that was in point.

ALR, ALR 2d, and *ALR* 3d (if you want to be camp refer to the set by its full name) have word indexes that lead you to annotations, tables of cases to those cases reprinted in full, and digest numbers (the term "key" belongs to West, but the idea is the same). The Total-Client Service offered by this publisher would fill a sizable den with multi-colored books that make fine backgrounds for group pictures.

With these two publishers, any intelligent person can become a tradesman at the law, but he would be inconvenienced if I neglected a few more tools.

First, I recommend Law Reviews. Why should a legal researcher want to read what some law professor, secluded from the rigors and challenges of practice, has to say about a judge's aptitude in applying the law to the facts? The truth is that some judges do not write clearly, others not well, and a few not wisely, which in all fairness must be said about some who write for law reviews. All law reviews have an entré in the *Index to Legal Peri-*

odicals which will lead you to articles on the point you wish to research. Two things should be mentioned about law reviews: one is that they frequently exorcise, constantly revisit, and occasionally "lay a ghost to rest." However do not let these titles frighten you or make you think the subject is too lively for law. The second point is that Justice Holmes once observed that he was not disturbed when a law review disagreed with him, it was when it agreed with him that he was troubled.

If it were not for Jerry Giesler, a once prominent Hollwood lawyer, I would neglect *Shepard's*. In his entertaining autobiography Mr. Giesler recounts how he lost a case because he did not Shepardize it. In his words to Shepardize meant "not only following through on your cases to see what happened to them when they were appealed to a higher court, but following them even further, to find out whether those decisions had been sustained or reversed by subsequent decisions." It has been said that the Lawyers' Psalm begins "The Shepard is my Lord."

Of course this short survey cannot acquaint one with all the legal tools which fill the student's tool box to overflowing; but then again, most of them are forgotten as time recedes and the waist line increases. There are encyclopedias, loose-leaf services, treatises, bar association publications, and even a Law Research Service that will do research for lawyers by use of a computer. To become familiar with these, I recommend Roalfe on *How to Find the Law* and Price and Bitner on *Effective Legal Research*. And one should not forget the oft-quoted statement of Sir Walter Scott that "A lawyer without history or literature is a mechanic, a mere working mason; if he possesses some knowledge of these, he may venture to call himself an architect."

With this background it is time for a trial run. Let us

say you want to know what your rights are to represent yourself in court. It goes without saying that one cannot practise law without a license, and only renegades like Jack Cade desire to do anything about this state of affairs. You simply go to the *Descriptive Word Index* of the Decennial Digest, select the word best befitting your situation and start your search. "Client" is fine and it will refer you to the major heading, "Attorney & Client." Under the latter, you find the sub-heading "Parties" which refers you to "Right to appear in person or by attorney. *Atty & C 62*." There in volume three (viz., *Attorney & Client 62*) of the Sixth Decennial Digest covering the years 1946-1956 you will find six columns of digested cases under this key number topic. With this beginning you can go backward and forward, until you find the cases you feel will be most helpful to you, i.e., consult the digests prior to 1946 and subsequent to 1956.

My research turned up the interesting case of *Heathman v. Hatch,* 372 Pacific Second 990 (Jan. 26, 1962), a Utah case. This case affirmed the principle of one's right to represent himself in court. However, this was a pyrrhic victory, as it was determined that although the plaintiff had every right to try his own case, he had neglected to state a cause of action. Thus, the plaintiff not only had the expense of starting his case all over again, but had to pay the costs of the case for wasting the time of the court and the defendant. The subject of pleading, which was this plaintiff's Waterloo (and there I go again with my metaphors), I have not discussed but I will say that most laymen who try their own cases remind one of the aspiring painter who did not know with which end of the brush to paint. Although this is no handicap in today's world of art, the use of avant-garde methods are frowned upon by the courts.

Despite this setback, dear law dictionary readers, hopefully you have learned a little law and, more important, you are aware of your cherished right to try your own case. May I conclude with that well-known aphorism, for which there is no key number: one who tries his own case has a fool for a client (See PLAINTIFF).

Edward J. Bander

ENGLISH LEGAL WORDS
TERMS AND PHRASES
A

ABET

To encourage another in the commission of a crime.

ACCESSORY

An active participant in a crime by reason of participating only in its preliminaries (accessory before the fact) or in furthering its success (accessory after the fact).

ACCOMMODATION

An accommodation involves an accommodated party, or a person whose credit may involve a risk; and an accommodation party, or one who is willing to sign his name to an accommodation paper (a promissory note) and thereby stand good to the creditor (usually a bank) for any default. Its extra legal effect is to break up long standing friendships.

ACCOMPLICE

A partner in crime.

ACCORD AND SATISFACTION

The attempt at an efficacious settling of differances between parties involving some give and take.

ACQUIT

A legal determination of not guilty.

ACT

"But an act, which in itself is merely a voluntary muscular contraction, derives all its character from the consequences which will follow it under the circumstances in which it was done." 195 U.S. 194, 205 (1904).

ADJUSTED GROSS INCOME

Basically this is the gross income of an individual minus his business expenses.

ADMINISTRATIVE LAW

From humble beginnings in equity, administrative law has become a vast octupus creeping into all phases of our lives. Given life and sustenance by Congress, power and direction by the executive, limitations and hand-slapping by the courts, they cover areas as suggested by the following titles of a meager listing of the commissions: Federal Power Commission, Interstate Commerce Commission, Federal Communications Commission.

ADMINISTRATIVE PROCEDURE ACT

A Federal statute which establishes uniform rules of procedure for federal administrative agencies and makes it possible for those dealing with these agencies to be aware of their rights.

ADOPTION

A judicial proceeding establishing the relationship of child and parent between persons who are

2

not so related. Leavy, *The Law of Adoption* (Legal Almanac Series No. 3, 1954).

ADVISORY OPINION

An opinion rendered by an appellate court at the request of the government or an interested party that suggests how the court would rule should adversary litigation develop on a particular fact pattern. Some State courts will give an advisory opinion; the United States Supreme Court will not.

AFFIDAVIT

A sworn statement in writing taken before a notary.

AFFIRM

The holding of an upper court that the ruling of an inferior court shall stand. For example, the Federal District Court in Massachusetts is inferior (only in the sense of power) to the United States Court of Appeals for the First Circuit; and the adjudications of the District Court, when appealed to the Court of Appeals, can be affirmed, overruled, etc.

AGENT

One who acts in the interests of another, called a principal. The principal can be held responsible for the acts of the agent, and the usual question is whether the agent was acting within the scope of his responsibilities.

3

ALIMONY

Support payments made after a divorce or legal separation. Alimony and separate maintenance payments to a wife are deductible so far as income tax goes; but child support payments are not. As to the latter, however, an exemption can be claimed.

AMORTIZATION

Generally, the building up of a sinking fund, through periodic payments, for the purpose of paying off an obligation when it becomes due in the future, such as a mortgage. In tax law it means obtaining tax deductions over a period of years for money already spent on a capital investment.

ANNOTATION

In law this usually means a commercial explanation of the significance of a court decision. *The American Law Reports, Third Series,* reprints leading state and lower federal court decisions and follows them with an explanation of the law in the case reviewed, how other states have handled this type of case and other pertinent information. *The Lawyers Edition* of the United States Supreme Court Reports will take a case such as *Brown v. Board of Education,* the school segregation case, and show the tortuous route by which the Court arrived at its decision, touching on significant precedents, such as *Plessy v. Ferguson,* and statutes that give the complete background to the case.

ANNUITIES

Some insurance policies provide for periodic payments or annuities, after the policy has matured. If your employer made the payments on the policy, you are taxable onthe full amount; otherwise you pay a tax on a percentage of the annuity according to a formula acceptable to the Internal Revenue Bureau.

ANSWER

The plaintiff's declaration sets out his grievances for which he seeks relief at law. The defendant's answer is just that, usually suggesting to the court that no action at law lies. In theory and in practice, pleadings such as these are designed to get to the bone of contention between the parties.

ANTITRUST LAWS

An extensive body of law, felt by many to be in utter disarray, which attempts to outlaw restraint of trade and efforts at monopolization of industry. The major antitrust acts are the Sherman Act, the Clayton Act and the Federal Trade Commission Act.

APPEAL

The removal of a case, by the losing party, from a lower court to one of superior jurisdiction for the purpose of obtaining a review.

APPELLANT

See PLAINTIFF

APPELLEE

See PLAINTIFF

APPORTIONMENT

Baker v. Carr, 369 U.S. 186 (1962) is the land-mark case in this field. Where, in one state, a rural Congressional District of 20,000 elects one Congressman; and a city Congressional District of 200,000 elects one Congressman; it is a clear instance of bad apportionment. Congressional districting is concerned with the election of United States Congressmen (not Senators), while state districting has to do with the election of state officials. Those who feel the districting is unfair clamor for reapportionment and "one man-one vote;" those who are satisfied with the status quo say the courts should not interfere in the "political thicket"; in other words, courts should avoid matters that involve more politics than law. We live by symbols and shibboleths.

APPURTENANT

Attached.

ARBITRATION

When the disputing parties agree to abide by the decision of a neutral party, arbitration has taken place. Compulsory arbitration is where the law steps in and requires arbitration whether or not it was contemplated by the disputing parties.

ARRANGEMENT

Any plan of the debtor for the payment of his unsecured debts that, if not acceptable, may lead to bankruptcy. See 11 U.S.C. section 706 (1).

ASSIGN

Where A agrees to pay B a particular sum, in a valid contract, B can assign this benefit to C. B becomes the assignor and C the assignee. Assignments can be very tricky and readers are advised to consult a lawyer less they be morally, civilly and criminally in error.

ASYLUM

The refusal of a sovereign to extradite a citizen of another country.

B

BAIL

A person awaiting trial can usually be released if he will post a certain amount of money to guarantee that he will appear for trial This is known as being "out on bail." In practice, the defendant borrows the money from a professional bondsman, and many believe present bail procedures to be historically unsound, an undue imposition on those least able to pay, and an affront to a civilized society.

BAILMENT

If A agrees to permit B's bull to graze in his pasture, A is a bailee and B is a bailor and the transaction is a bailment. Resulting negligence depends on whom a benefit is being conferred. Thus, if A has a cow, it may alter circumstances.

BANKRUPTCY

The last resort of liquidation. All assets are turned over to the court and distributed to the creditors. The debtor is then discharged from all financial obligations and he is free to run the same course again in due time.

BENEFICIARY

One who benefits from a legal transaction such as a will, a trust or an agreement. The distinctive feature of a beneficiary is that he can receive

a legally enforcible benefit for no legally enforcible reason.

BEQUEST

A gift under a will. Most charitable foundations
can supply you with a sample form of a bequest.

BILL

A bill becomes a law in the United States when
it is passed by both houses of Congress and,
with a major exception, signed by the President.
These laws, when first published, are called
slip laws and become part of a set called the
Statutes at Large. The *United States Code* ar-
ranges the public laws that are in force by title,
thereby providing a convenient means of re-
searching the law. There are innumerable commercial publications that facilitate research in
this field: Commerce Clearing House *Congressional Index; Congressional Quarterly, United
States Code Annotated* and the *United States
Code Congressional and Administrative News*.

BILL OF RIGHTS

The first ten amendments of the United States
Constitution, which limit the powers of the Federal Government. Recent Supreme Court decisions have indicated that most of these rights are
available to the citizen against the state as well
as the Federal Government.

BLUE SKY LAWS

State regulation protecting the gullible public
from buying lots in fee simple in the blue sky.

See SECURITIES. See, Loss & Cowett, *Blue Sky Law* (1958).

BOILER PLATE RATIFICATION

The blanket ratification of the acts of the directors and officers of a corporation by the shareholders.

BOYCOTT

In labor law, an attempt by organized labor to bring a company to its knees by refusing to work and discouraging people in the use of the recalcitrant company's products.

BRIEF

Written, formal arguments of counsel in support of a client's legal contentions. A Brandeis brief is one that requests the Court to consider data outside the law, such as statistics or health practices, in weighing the merits of a case. A brief *in forma pauperis* is one prepared, usually by a convict with permission of the court, in handwriting or typed, so as to avoid the prohibitive costs of printed briefs. See also *AMICUS CURIAE*.

BY-LAWS

Specific provisions supplementing the charters or constitutions of corporations, labor unions, universities, and other organizations.

C

CALENDAR

This can mean the order in which cases are to be heard during a term of court. *Martindale-Hubbell Law Directory* contains court calendars for all state and federal courts which lists pertinent information about the courts including the names of the judges, the names of the court, and the beginning of the term.

CANON

Usually associated with the laws of the Roman Catholic Church. There is also the canons of ethics which all lawyers must abide by, or be subject to disciplinary action by bar associations and possible disbarment by the state; and canons of judicial ethics which apply to the judiciary.

CAPITAL GAINS

An arbitrary formula that saves an inestimable amount of taxes to those most able to afford them. For instance, long-term capital gains, such as stocks, property, etc., are taxed at not more than 25%. See also PERCENTAGE DEPLETION.

CARRIER

A carrier is one who carries goods or people for profit. A railroad or an airline is a public

11

carrier and is thereby subject to both state and federal regulation.

CASE

In common parlance, a cause of action commenced in court. It is also a synonym for an opinion of the court, as in, "I am sorry, Professor, but I did not read that case."

CEASE AND DESIST ORDERS

The final order of an administrative agency to a respondent engaged in activities determined by the agency to be violative of the law. These orders can sometimes be located in the *Federal Register*; and some publishers, such as the Commerce Clearing House, issue loose-leaf services that keep abreast of these developments. An example is the CCH *Trade Regulation Reporter*.

CHARGE

Usually a summing up to the jury of the law in the case by the trial judge. Counsel can suggest charges for the court to make and can appeal on the basis of the incorrectness of a charge. The publication of books listing judicially—tried charges, and the growing exchange of information among judges at seminars have taken the dramatic sting out of this aspect of the trial.

CHARTER

The early history of our country was that of a commercial body operating a colony under a charter from the King. Corporations usually operate under a charter from the State. The charter spells out the limits under which the corporate body can act and any change of intention must be approved by the stockholders or by whatever provisions are provided for in the charter or by the State. The *Dartmouth College Case* is probably the most famous case involving a charter.

A charter can also be an *ad hoc* hiring of a means of transportation. Thus a charter airline is one that cannot run on a schedule but must be chartered for a specific purpose.

CHATTEL MORTGAGE

A has ten bushels of wheat. He wants to borrow $100 from B. B agrees to give A $100 and as security has A sign the wheat over to him. If A fails to pay B, B owns the wheat. In other words, it is usually a signed agreement of personal property (not land), for purposes of obtaining money, credit or services. The problem of title is important, particularly in bankruptcy cases. It can mean the difference between getting the wheat or ten cents on the dollar.

CHECK

An instrument or draft drawn on a bank and payable on demand. The depositor draws on his account at the bank, usually signs in the lower right hand corner of the check and is referred to as the drawer of the check. The bank is the drawee. The payee (who can also be a "holder" and a "bearer") is the party to whom the check is paid "to the order of." An indorser of a check is one who signs on the back of the check; with words of limitation, if he pleases, such as "pay only to . . .;" and to whom the drawee bank will pay the amount specified in the check. A holder in due course of a check can be the payee or an indorser. A certified check is one that the bank has no choice but to accept the check. The UNI-FORM LAWS ANNOTATED contains two volumes devoted to the UNIFORM COMMERCIAL CODE which succinctly and with examples explain the above terms.

CIRCUIT COURT

The United States Court of Appeals for the Second Circuit has federal jurisdiction over New York, Vermont and Connecticut. It hears appeals from the federal district courts within its jurisdiction. There are ten other Courts of Appeal that blanket the United States and its possessions. Appeals from the Courts of Appeal are taken to the United States Supreme Court.

State court systems usually follow the pattern of trial court, intermediate appellate court and high court which have their basis in the old circuit court systems. In the old days, judges had to make their circuits on horseback and judicial appointments were not quite as sought after as they are today.

CITATION

In a brief, one cites cases and authorities that support a legal position. To determine whether a case is good authority one consults a citator. Here the citing case is the one that you want to check to make sure it is still authoritative; and cited cases are those that have used the citing case in its reasoning. If *Jones v. James*, 100 Mass. 89(1911) (the citing case) contains law favorable to your side the citator would reveal subsequent cases (cited cases) that referred back to it (i.e., 200 Mass. 21 may overrule it). Cited cases follow in time the citing case and thus can overrule it. *Shepard* citators are an indispensable aid in following the vagaries of citing cases in courts of law.

CIVIL ACTION

When one sues in tort or contract, one is bringing a civil action. On the other hand, a criminal action involves an action by the state against one violating its laws.

CLEAR AND PRESENT DANGER RULE

"The question in every case is whether the words used are used in such circumstances and are of such a nature as to create a clear and present danger that they will bring about the substantive evils that Congress has a right to prevent," Holmes, J., *Schenck v. U.S.*, 249 U.S. 47, 52 (1919). Justice Holmes's doctrine has since been whittled down but freedom of speech owes much to its enunciation.

CLOSE CORPORATION

Also known as family corporations, they are characterized by the close identity of both ownership and management, the shares are not usually listed or quoted on the exchanges, and their financial affairs can be kept tight to the vest.

CLOSED SHOP

An agreement between an employer and a union to hire only union members.

CODIFICATION

To codify the laws of a state. The practical effect of a codification is to eliminate archaic expressions, arrange the law in force by subject matter and rewrite unclear and poorly drawn passages. To some extent this is being done by the RESTATEMENT, MODEL CODES and UNIFORM STATE LAWS.

COLLATERAL

Any security given for a debt. A bank book surrendered to the loaning bank is collateral for the loan.

COLLECTIVE BARGAINING

Basically, the democratic right of management and labor to hammer out an agreement without outside interference. Like all rights it is not absolute and in times of emergency the government does interfere. Rachlin, *Labor Law* (Legal Almanac Series No. 7, 1961).

COMITY

The courtesy of one state or nation recognizing the laws of another state or nation. This should not be confused with "full faith and credit" which, in the Constitution of the United States, obliges one state to follow the law, albeit with its eyes open, of the other states. Mexican and Reno divorces are recognized, in the former instance, by comity; in the latter, by full faith and credit.

COMMERCE POWER

The Constitution says that "Congress shall have the power to regulate commerce . . . among the several States, . . ." and on this pretext or mandate, depending on one's view, Congress has had its say in the regulation of social and economic conditions that is far ranging.

COMMON LAW

The bulwark of our judicial system. "The common law consists of a few broad and comprehensive principles, founded on reason, natural justice, and enlightened public policy, modified and adapted to the circumstances of all the particular cases which fall within it." Shaw, J., 1 Gray 263 (1845).

COMMUNITY PROPERTY

In Arizona, California, Idaho, Louisiana, Nevada, New Mexico, Texas and Washington both spouses have a common ownership in their mutual posessions. In divorce, the community property may be divided equally or as the court sees fit.

COMPANY UNION

An unaffiliated union whose membership is limited to the employees of a single company. To rank and file union members it is a term of opprobium.

COMPOSITION

The acceptance by a creditor of something less than the full value of his debt rather than take the chance of even less acceptable terms forcing the debtor into bankruptcy.

CONCUR

In judicial opinions, where a judge agrees with the majority view but does not wish to be associated with it. He generally adds words of qualification.

CONCURRENT JURISDICTION

When more than one court can hear a particular cause. In many instances, such as in labor and bankruptcy, the litigants have a choice as to whether they prefer a state or federal court to determine their cause. But see PREEMPT.

CONDITIONAL SALE

A wants to sell B's toy airplanes. He agrees to pay $50 down and pay the rest in installments, title to the airplanes to remain in A until full payment. The transaction is similar to a chattel mortgage. The significant point is that the vendor (A) retains title and the vendee (B) has the goods.

CONFLICT OF LAWS

In many instances, State A will determine the rights between parties according to the law of State B. Conflicts of this type are inevitable, and a set of rules, not always understandable and frequently quibbled over by scholars, have grown so as to guide courts as to which law they should apply in certain circumstances.

CONGLOMERATE MERGER

This type of merger involves both HORIZON-TAL and VERTICAL MERGERS.

CONSIDERATION

Value given or promised. See CONTRACT.

CONSIGNMENT

A consignor gives up his goods but not his ownership of the goods to a consignee. Ideally, the consignee sells the goods, pays the consignor a stipulated amount and pockets the excess. The desired legal effect, of course, is that the consignment cannot be attached by a creditor of the consignee. The consignee also need not sell the entire consignment, but can return that which remains unsold.

CONSPIRACY

Probably the vaguest term in all criminal law. It is an agreement betwen two or more persons to violate the law. There are conspiracies to rob a bank, conspiracies in restraint of trade, and many others.

CONSTITUTION

The fundamental law of a nation; written, as in the United States, unwritten, as in England.

CONTINGENT FEE

A legal arrangement between an attorney and his client, most prevalent in automobile claims, where the attorney does not receive compensation unless he obtains a settlement worthy of division. It is to be confused with champerty, which is an illegal arrangement with the same division in mind.

CONTRACT

A basic right, fraught with exceptions, limitations and qualifications to enter into an agreement, for a consideration, with another party to do or not to do just about anything under the sun. In student language a contract is generally broken up into an offer and an acceptance. See TORT. Wincor, *Law of Contracts* (Legal Almanac Series No. 36, 1954).

CONVENTION

An agreement between two or more nations. An example is the Universal Copyright Convention which affords protection of an author's work in all the countries which have signed the Convention.

CONVERSION

Prosser says that this tort defies definition but

any serious invasion of an owner's property is a conversion. A clear case of a converter is a purchaser, however innocent, of stolen goods.

CONVEYANCE

A transfer of interest in land involves an assurance that the grantor has title, that there has been an execution and delivery of a valid instrument of conveyance, and that the deed (or other instrument of conveyance) has been recorded in accordance with the terms of the recording act of the state concerned. The grantor is the person who wants to sell property and the grantee is the one who wants to buy it.

CONVICTION

The result of a criminal trial which ends in the judge declaring the defendant guilty.

COOPERATIVE

Essentially an association of individuals banded together for economic reasons such as cooperative buying. They need not be incorporated, although it can be advantageous as in cooperative apartment house ownership. There can be tax advantages in cooperatives as opposed to incorporating.

COPYRIGHT

A statutory grant protecting an author from having his published work published without his authority. In the United States the maximum protection is fifty-six years. "The person to whom it is given has invented some new collocation of visible or audible points, - of lines, colors, sounds, or words." 209 U.S. 1, 19 (1908). Wincor, *How to Secure Copyright* (Legal Almanac Series No. 21, 1957).

CORPORATION

"The corporation is legally distinct from its members, and its debts are not their debts. Therefore, when a paid-up share in a corporation is taken, no liability is assumed, apart from statute, but simply a right equal in value to a corresponding share in the assets and good will of the concern after its debts are paid." 202 U.S. 295 (300).

COURT MARTIAL

Military personnel are tried before court martial courts for offenses against military law. There is no jury.

COURT OF LAST RESORT

The end of the line for a litigant. In many instances the end of the line can be the court of first instance. There is no constitutional right to be heard by the United States Supreme Court or even the highest court of a state.

COVENANT

A promise under seal to do or to refrain from doing a specified thing. There are covenants against encumbrances, covenants of quiet enjoyment, and covenants running with the land.

CREDIT UNIONS

An effort by groups having a common interest, sometimes ethnic, sometimes having a common employer, to save and borrow money at beneficial rates.

CREDITOR

A person who has a legally enforcible claim for money against another person, called the debtor. The bills that you receive the first of the month are from creditors.

CRIME

Either a misdemeanor or a felony.

D

DAMAGES

The amount of money, usually plus interest, recovered in a court of law as compensation to the party bringing the action for the harm done. Exemplary or punitive damages, such as in libel and slander cases, are awarded as a punishment to the defendant and an example to the public. Treble damages, such as that written into our antitrust law, mean just that. Nominal damages are awarded where the jury recognizes the plaintiff is right, but foolhardily so.

DEBENTURES

Generally a bond of indebtedness of a corporation which will be paid off only so long as the corporation has funds, i.e. it is an unsecured debt or one not backed by collateral.

DEBT

An obligation to pay a specified sum of money. See CREDITOR.

DECEDENT

One who did not take it with him and is spared seeing who is going to get it.

DECISION

The determination at a court of law as to who won the case.

DECREE

Most frequently heard of in divorce actions where the court spells out who gets the custody, visitation rights and alimony. In administrative agencies there are consent decrees where a corporation consents to act in a particular manner and thus end the litigation against it.

DEDUCTIONS

Schedule C of Tax Form 1040 lists the deductions that can be taken that are due to running your business or profession. There are also deductions that can be taken for medical expenses, charitable contributions, taxes, etc. The taxpayer should be reminded that business deductions are subtracted to make up the ADJUSTED GROSS INCOME, i.e. they are not part of your tax.

DEED

Basically a means of transferring title to land from one person to another. See CONVEYANCE.

DEFAMATION

A generic term covering both LIBEL and SLANDER.

DEFAULT

In debts and mortgages, it denotes a failure to pay as stipulated by the parties in the original agreement. The consequences were never as fearful as the old melodramas led us to believe.

A defendant in an action who refuses to enter proper pleadings can be found liable, and a judgment entered against him, without the case being determined on its merits. The law is not patient with those who sit on their rights.

DEFENDANT

See PLAINTIFF

DELEGATION OF POWERS

Nice constitutional questions can arise when Congress delegates to the President or an administrative agency the right to act as if Congress itself were acting. Necessity is usually the mother of delegation.

DELIBERATE SPEED

A term used by the Supreme Court to carry out a program of desegregation in Southern schools. Its first appearance in a Supreme Court case was in 222 U.S. 17, 19, 20 (1911).

DEMURRER

The answer of the defendant to the plaintiff's allegation that even assuming everything the plaintiff said could be substantiated he would have no cause of action against the defendant.

DENIAL

As opposed to a demurrer, the denial frames the issues to be litigated. If A claims B owes him one thousand dollars and B denies it, the jury now can hear evidence on the matter.

DEPOSITION

A pretrial procedure where a party to a suit, or a witness, or one who may not be able to appear at the trial, is ordered to give testimony under oath (an affidavit) that may be used at the trial. The person giving the testimony is called a deponent.

DEPRECIATION

A diminuation in value or price. For income tax purposes, you are allowed a deduction for the gradual obsolescence of equipment purchased for use in business.

DERIVATIVE ACTION

In corporation law, those who stand to benefit from a corporation's profits, can sue on behalf of the corporation to influence those who are guiding its destinies. At times, these suits are nothing more than nuisance suits, which are encouraged by corporations who settle rather than fight them, to the detriment of those stockholders not involved in the litigation.

DEVISE

One of the redundancies of lawyers in wills is "to devise and bequeath" when the latter term is sufficient to leave property by will.

DISCRIMINATION

It is not an evil to be discriminating in one's taste, but when the term is used in the sense of violating a statute or the sense of the Constitution it can bring down the full might of our government upon the offender. Race, creed, union membership or sex can be examples of the latter.

DISSENT

See OPINION.

DISSOLUTION

In corporate law, the termination of a corporation's existence. For this and other corporate terms and textual treatment see Hornstein, *Corporation Law and Practice* (1959 with supplements).

DISTRICTING

"The process of drawing the final lines by which each legislative district is bounded" whereas "APPORTIONMENT has ordinarily been described as the allocation of legislative seats by a legislative body to a subordinate unit of government." McKay, *Reapportionment* 6 (1965).

DIVIDENDS

A division of a corporation's assets, to the amount determined by the corporation, to its stockholders. For types of dividends, See West's McKinney's Forms: *Business Corporation Law, Glossary of Corporate Terms* (1965).

DIVORCE

The act of rendering asunder a male and a female previously bound together by a solemn ceremony of marriage committing them to union until death do them part. Most states will not grant a divorce unless there is legal fault on the part of one spouse. The modern view is to provide a conciliation service, and, where reconciliation is impossible, grant a divorce by, in effect, consent. Kuchler, *The Law of Marriage and Divorce* (Legal Almanac Series No. 1 1961).

DOCKET

This is the formal record maintained by the clerk of court that indicates, in abbreviated form, the pleadings filed, the time of trial and the determination of the court. The dockets are a public record and available to the public. Many commercial enterprises are designed to facilitate docket research for the practising lawyer. In New York there is the *New York Law Journal* and for the Supreme Court of the United States there is the *United States Law Week*.

DOE, JOHN

The fictitious plaintiff in the old action of ejectment.

DOMICILE

The legal distinction between domicile and residence eludes this compiler and has been the cause of much spilt ink, double taxation and quite a few bastards in instances where a man was lulled into thinking he had been successfully

29

divorced. Candidates for office must take this
term seriously. Basically it indicates that address
a man calls his home. "The very meaning of
domicile is the technically preeminent headquar-
ters that every person is compelled to have in
order that certain rights and duties that have
been attached to it by the law may be determined." 232 U.S. 619, 625 (1914).

DRAFT

An order for the payment of money drawn by
A (the drawer) ordering B (the drawee) to pay
a sum of money to C (the payee). Thus C obtains the money, B provides the cash, and A has
the assets.

DRAFT LAW

The Selective Training and Service Act of 1940
and the Selective Service Act of 1948 are examples, like rent control, of emergency legislation
that shall probably follow us to the grave.

DRAWEE

See CHECK.

DRAWER

See CHECK.

DUAL NATIONALITY

A citizen of two states.

DUE PROCESS OF LAW

A term found in the Fifth and Fourteenth Amendments to the Constitution and also in the Constitutions of many states. "Those fundamental notions of fairness and justice in the determination of guilt or innocence which lie imbedded in the feelings of the American people. . ." 332 U.S. 596, 607 (1948).

DURESS

Many transactions on their face appear to be legally enforcible, but if the use of force, physically and even emotionally, was employed to bring them about, courts will turn their backs on them.

E

EASEMENT

An easement is a privilege without profit that the owner of one estate in land (called a tenement by lawyers), by reason of such ownership, has a right to enjoy over another estate in land for a special purpose not inconsistent with a general property in the owner. Practically this can mean that A can have a right of way over B's land such as passing over it so as to get onto a highway. The dominant tenement is the one that enjoys the privilege (A); the subservient tenement is stuck with a provision that will naturally affect its market value.

EMBEZZLEMENT

This crime is usually associated with bank officials and bailors who appropriate goods entrusted to them so that the wrongful act is subsequent to their receiving the property. Larceny is simply a wrongful appropriation from the word go. The former is considered a white-collar crime and the latter is associated with the less newsworthy indigents.

EMINENT DOMAIN

The right of the State to take private property for public purposes. See POLICE POWER.

ENDORSEMENT

See CHECK.

ENJOIN

An injunction or order by a court that can require specific conduct of a person, such as limiting the number of cats he can care for in his residence or to refrain from carrying a sign, "Jones Car Agency Sold Me A Lemon."

ENTIRETY

A tenancy by the entirety is where husband and wife own jointly. It is a type of joint tenancy.

EQUAL PROTECTION CLAUSE

A clause of the Fourteenth Amendment that between 1886 and the 1930's was invoked to prohibit unreasonable state regulation in economic and social matters but has lately been invoked to protect individual rights in such areas as racial discrimination and apportionment. See 37 Calif. L. Rev. 341 (1949).

EQUITY

The distinction between courts of equity and courts of law is a sublime mixture of English history and human nature. Law is necessary, equity is practical and we must have both or we will have neither. In law you ask for damages for breach of contract; in equity you ask for specific performance of the contract. In law you can demand your rights, rascal though you be; in equity you must be honorable or at least come into court with clean hands. In equity you can abate a nuisance, stop a profligate heir from wasting an inheritance, and so on.

ESCROW

A wishes to sell his house to B but not until B raises $5000. B wants some kind of a guarantee that A will go through with the deal after he raises the money. The necessary instruments of sale are put in the hands of a bank, or, as is said, in escrow, and when B raises the money the transaction can be completed. The third person need not be a bank.

ESTOPPEL

Where one has by deeds or words created an image of himself, he cannot then come into court and picture himself differently. A sells T goods as P's agent. He is not and P knows it. P delivers the goods. T pays A. A absconds. P can be estopped from saying A was not his agent, and therefore T had no right to pay A.

EVIDENCE

Wigmore on *Evidence* is a bulky ten-volume set that advises lawyers what they can and cannot do in a court of law to best present their client's case.

EXCEPTION

During the course of a trial, where counsel objects to a ruling of the court and is overruled, counsel than takes exception to the ruling and has something to put into the record should he lose the case and wish to appeal.

EXCLUSIVE DEALING

Illegal arrangements by buyers and sellers to deal in a preferential way with one another and thus weaken those competing for similar business.

EXECUTOR (male) EXECUTRIX (female)

A person named in a will to carry out its terms. The usual procedure is to appoint a trusted friend and a bank or trust company as executors.

EXEMPT

A tax-exempt foundation is one that does not have to pay taxes.

EXPATRIATION

The renunciation of nationality by an individual. See Hale, *Man Without A Country*.

EXPENSES

There are a wide variety of expenses that are deductile for income tax purposes. See DEDUCTIONS. There are many that are not, such as personal expenses. The play, Any Wednesday is an example of the arbitrariness of the guidelines, where a businessman was able to maintain a mistress as a business expense.

EXTRADITION

"For while of course a man is not to be sent from the country merely upon demand or surmise, yet if there is presented, even in somewhat untechnical form according to our ideas, such reasonable ground to suppose him guilty as to make it proper that he should be tried, good faith to the demanding government requires his surrender." 221 U.S. 508, 512 (1908).

F

F.O.B.

This means that the seller takes all risks until the goods reach a designation named.

FACTOR

A type of agent who transacts business for a principal.

FAIR MARKET VALUE

A figure that the court will accept as the going value for a piece of property.

FEDERAL ANALOGY

The concept that a state need not apportion one of its legislatures according to population because the United States Senate is chosen on a geographical rather than a population basis. See APPORTIONMENT and DISTRICTING.

FELONY

In New York State and elsewhere an offense for which a sentence to a term of imprisonment in excess of one year is authorized by law.

FIDUCIARY

A person, such as an executor or a receiver in bankruptcy, who is entrusted with the property of others. As an executor of a will he must see to it that the intentions of the testator are carried out, that the expenses are necessary and accurate, that the money is properly invested until disbursed, etc.

FORECLOSURE

The forced sale of mortgaged property, from which the proceeds are given to the mortgagor.

FULL FAITH AND CREDIT

See COMITY.

G

GARNISHMENT

The usual procedure is for the creditor to get a court order requiring the debtor's employer to set aside a stipulated amount from the debtor-employee's salary to be used to diminish the existing debt. The debtor is called a garnishee.

GENOCIDE

The attempt to destroy a national, ethic or religious group such as the Nazi effort to destroy the Jews.

GIFT

A valid transfer of property without consideration or compensation by the party receiving it. Gifts are not taxable.

GRAND JURY

A body of men, the number of whom varies in different jurisdictions, sworn to inquire into crimes within the jurisdiction of the county or district.

GRANTEE

See CONVEYANCE.

GRANTOR

See CONVEYANCE.

GROSS INCOME

All income subject to be taxed is called gross income. Those who tamper with gross income become tax evaders and go to jail; those who tamper after listing gross income are tax avoiders and go to Florida.

GUARANTEE CLAUSE

The United States Constitution in Article IV, section four guarantees the states a Republican form of government.

GUARANTY

A guarantor is one who agrees to answer for the debt of another, i.e., A sells goods to B only because C stands behind B. C is a guarantor.

GUARDIAN

A court appointed individual appointed to act in the interests of one legally not capable of acting for himself. Infants, the insane, the senile are the usual wards of a guardian. Mackay, *Guardianship and the Protection of Infants* (Legal Almanac Series No. 6, 1957).

GUILTY

A determination that the defendant has committed the crime as charged.

H

HEARING

Extensively employed by administrative agencies, they are adjudicative proceedings, usually
held in public, employing judicial safeguards
and followed by a decision which can be appealed in a court of law. Many believe that administrative agencies should not have an adjudicative function, and one labor law authority
has gone so far as to advocate abolishment of the
National Labor Relations Board, adjudicative
and administrative.

HEARSAY

A rule of evidence that a witness cannot repeat
the words of another but only relate what he
himself has observed. The exceptions to this
rule are numerous, the apparent guide being
common sense.

HEIR

In today's usage, it means one who takes real
and personal property by intestate succession,
that is, in a given situation, a son who inherits
his share of his father's property on the death of
the father. It is not proper to speak of heirs of a
living person nor can a dog have heirs.

HORIZONTAL MERGER

The union of several corporations engaged in
the same business for the purpose of operating
as one business.

I

IMMUNITY

One who is exempt from the ordinary workings of the law. Members of Congress are privileged from arrest during sessions and a party to a crime can be granted immunity from prosecution for turning state's evidence.

IMPEACH

During the course of a trial, a witness's credibility can be impeached by showing he lied. There were two unsuccessful impeachments of high public officials: President Andrew Johnson and Supreme Court Justice Samuel Chase. Impeachment proceedings, which are attempts to remove an official from high public office for misconduct, are governed by the United States Constitution for federal officials and by state constitutions for state officials.

IMPLIED

A contract implied in fact is one where the conduct of the parties brings the court to an inescapable deduction. A contract implied in law is one where past experience puts its infallible stamp on present conduct. There are also implied powers, which is that controversal area in the operation of governments and corporations, that permit conduct nowhere granted in words but are obvious to those exercising them and a source of irritation to those, who, were they in power, would imply otherwise.

INCHOATE

Incomplete. To say choate would be to say couth.

INCOME

Taxable income includes compensation for services (wages, tips, etc.), interest, dividends, profits from sales, gains from capital assets, etc.

INCUMBRANCE

Anything that diminishes the value of land. An EASEMENT is an incumbrance. Also a MORT-GAGE.

INDEMNIFY

A good example of this is the contract of insurance, where an insurance company agrees to indemnify a party against some risk for a stipulated fee.

INDEMNITY

Where a party to a contract agrees to indemnify and hold harmless a second party from any damages arising out of the contract. A tenant is usually called upon to indemnify a landlord for any damages done during the course of the lease.

INDICIA OF OWNERSHIP

A significant indication of ownership to give

rise to legal obligations, i.e. the appearance of ownership.

INDICTMENT

A formal and written accusation of a crime against one or more persons presented by a grand jury under oath. What follows is an arraignment, where the defendant pleads guilty or not guilty, an opportunity to obtain counsel, the selection of a jury, the trial, the finding of the jury, appeals and sentencing. See Karlen, *The Citizen in Court* (1964).

INDIGENT IN COURT

There is a growing awarement that the indigent accused cannot possibly be aware of their rights under law and the Supreme Court, in recent years, has put the onus on enforcement officials to see to it that the poor are guided through the legal process without incriminating themselves. Compare Mr. Dooley: "Don't I think a poor man has a chanst in court? Iv coorse he has. He has the same chanst there that he has outside. He has a splendid poor man's chanst."

INDORSE

See CHECK.

INFORMATION

In an indictment, the jury returns an information; in an information, the district attorney makes the accusation. See INDICTMENT.

INJUNCTION

See ENJOIN.

INSANITY

A person cannot be tried for a crime if he is adjudged insane. The famous *M'Naghten* case puts it thusly: ". . . the party accused was laboring under such a defect of reason, from disease of the mind, as not to know the nature and quality of the act he was doing; or, if he did know it, that he did not know he was doing what was wrong." The rule has been severely criticized but seems to outlast its critics.

INSOLVENT

One who is unable to pay his debts as they fall due in the normal course of trade or business.

INSTRUCTION

See CHARGE.

INTENT

"If a man intentionally adopts certain conduct in certain circumstances known to him, and that conduct is forbidden by the law under those circumstances, he intentionally breaks the law in the only sense in which the law ever considers intent." 206 U.S. 246, 257 (1907).

INTERLOCUTORY

In divorce proceedings an interlocutory decree grants a divorce but does not make it final until a specific period of time has elapsed. During this period the parties to the divorce are legally separated but may not marry.

INTERNAL REVENUE BUREAU

The Federal agency charged with the duty to collect taxes.

INTERNATIONAL LAW

A body of rules governing the relations between states. These rules come from treaties, conventions, court decisions and many other sources.

INTERROGATORIES

Questions directed to the parties and witnesses in a civil action and which are answered under oath and in writing. They are designed to pinpoint the issues to be tried. Interrogatories follow the bringing of the action and can be used during the course of the trial.

INTESTATE

One who dies without leaving a will.

ISSUE

A term that can be very technical but basically means all the descendants of a person; sons, daughters, grandchildren, etc.

J

JEOPARDY

The term double jeopardy means that a person cannot be tried for the same crime twice.

JOINDER

The joining together of parties or causes of actions so· that the matter can be settled once and for all.

JOINT RETURN

A means of income-splitting for spouses.

JUDGMENT

The judgment is the final determination of a court of a specific case. Of course the judgment may be appealed and reversed by a higher court.

JUDICIAL REVIEW

The power of the United States Supreme Court to declare an act of Congress unconstitutional. This doctrine was established by Chief Justice John Marshall in the case of *Marbury v. Madison*, 5 U.S. (1 Church) 137 (1803).

JUDICIARY

Under our system of government there are the executive, embodied by our President, the legislative, embodied by Congress, and the judiciary, embodied by our courts. This balance of power among the three is written into the Constitution and there are many who feel that of the three, the courts are the least dangerous branch.

JURAT

Subscribed and sworn to me before this .... day of ...., 19 ....

John Q. Notary
Notary Public.

My commission expires January 10, 1972.

The above, with a notarial seal, is a jurat and can be found on all affidavits in this general form.

JURISDICTION

"Simply means that the Court finds the government in fact asserting its authority over the territory and will follow its lead . . . Jurisdiction is power and matter of fact." 248 U.S. 413, 419 (1919).

JURISPRUDENCE

The science of law. Theories of jurisprudence have been associated with many great names in the law. John Austin is associated with analytical jurisprudence, Hens Kelsen with the pure science of law, and Roscoe Pound with the sociological school of jurisprudence, to name but three.

JURY

In criminal law a jury consists of twelve persons

and they have been known to bring in a verdict in the teeth of both the law and the fact. In civil cases there have been constant pressures to cut down on the size of the jury, to accept a majority rather than a unanimous vote, and to abolish the institution altogether. But like other venerable institutions it will probably be here long after the automobile ceases to pose a threat to its stable operation.

JUSTICE

Fiat justitia, ruat coelum (Let justice be done, though the heavens may fall).

L

LANDLORD AND TENANT

The landlord is the lessor who grants to the tenant-lessee a right to possession of the property but not ownership. In New York City the usual lease runs for three years. The lease sets the terms of possession such as the amount of the rent, the purpose for which the property can be used, etc. Kuchler, *Landlord, Tenant and Co-op Housing* (Legal Almanac Series No. 11, 1960).

LARCENY

See EMBEZZLEMENT.

LATENT

In products liability cases, such as an electric blanket that catches fire, counsel for the injured person argues that the defect was hidden and did not turn up until the damage was done.

LAW, RULE OF

"A principle or rule of conduct so established as to justify a prediction with reasonable certainty that it will be enforced by the courts if its authority is challenged is, then, for the purpose of our study, a principle or rule of law." Cardozo, *Growth of the Law.* "The last result of human wisdom acting upon human experience for the benefit of the public." Samuel Johnson.

50

LEASE

See LANDLORD AND TENANT.

LEGAL AID

In most states there are legal aid (or public defender) societies to assist those little able to afford legal fees. In many states, law students assist in the handling of cases. Bar associations also have Legal Referral services where legal advice can be obtained for a norminal fee. At times, courts appoint counsel, particularly in capital cases, and state funds pay the attorney; but this has been said to be of more value to the attorney than the defendant.

LEGISLATION

The acts of a legislature. See BILL.

LEGITIMATE

A person, who, in the eyes of the law, is the child of a married couple.

LESSEE AND LESSOR

See LEASE.

LIABLE

If you punch Jones in the eye, you will be liable for damages. Used in this sense it is a prediction of what course the law will take should you exercise your will.

LIBEL

"A libel is harmful on its face. If a man sees fit to publish manifestly hurtful statements concerning an individual, without other justification than exists for an advertisement or a piece of news, the usual principles of tort will make him liable, if the statements are false or are true only of someone else." 214 U.S. 185, 189, 90 (1909). Thomas, *The Law of Libel and Slander* (Legal Almanac Series No. 15, 1963).

LIEN

A lienor or creditor is one who holds a lien on the property of another. The debtor or lienee holds the property on which there is a lien but, for a loan of money or some other consideration, acknowledges the title to be with the lienor. A mechanics' lien, a creature of statute, is where one who contracts to improve the land of another takes a lien upon the land as security for being paid. The reason for this precaution is that the debtor may have other creditors and a lienor has a high priority in getting paid.

LIQUIDATED

Damages that are fixed or settled according to an agreement by the parties should the terms of the contract not be fulfilled.

LITIGATION

A law suit, a judicial controversy, an action at law.

M

MAJORITARIANISM

Whereas majority rule implies all issues are decided by a mere plurality of numbers, majoritarianism qualifies that rule by insisting on a set of values, such as those incorporated in our Bill of Rights, which can not be tampered with irrespective of popular vote or public fancy.

MALICIOUS PROSECUTION

An action that lies in tort against a party who maliciously causes a criminal prosecution to be brought against a party. After the prosecution fails, this remedy is available to the maligned party.

MANDAMUS

A writ asking a court to order an official to carry out a public duty. In *Marbury v. Madison* (See JUDICIAL REVIEW), Chief Justice John Marshall was asked to order the Secretary of State Madison to give Mr. Marbury his commission as a magistrate.

MANDATORY

It is usually said that it is mandatory for a court to follow its past precedents whereas the decisions of courts of other states are only persuasive. See DICTUM.

MERGER

The joining of two or more corporations into one, all but one giving up their identification. When the joining together results in an entirely new corporation, you have a consolidation.

MISDEMEANOR

In New York State and elsewhere an offense, rather than a "traffic infraction," for which a sentence to a term of imprisonment in excess of fifteen days but not in excess of one year is authorized by law.

MITIGATE

If a newspaper libels a person and prints a retraction it can go far to mitigate or lessen damages. There are many applications of this principle in law.

MODEL CODES

The *Model Code of Evidence* and the work of Lewis Simes on probate and conveyancing are offered as guidelines for states and not uniform adoption as in UNIFORM STATE LAWS.

MOOT

If during the course of a trial nothing can be gained by permitting it to run its course, the reason for the trial becomes moot or meaningless. In law schools and national law school competitions, moot court arguments are held to test the skill of students.

MORTGAGE

A mortgagor is one who borrows money using his home or any other real property that he owns as security. The man who loans him the money is the mortgagee. The mortgagor has the advantage of the continued enjoyment of his property but, of course, will lose it if he does not repay the amount borrowed. The stipulations creating this situation is called a mortgage.

MOTION

Requests of counsel during the course of a trial are called motions. Examples of motions made during the course of a trial are motions to strike evidence, motions for a directed verdict and motions for a mistrial. There are also motions to correct a misleading record, to allow an amendment to the pleadings and many others.

MOTIVE

Although a man may have a motive, or a reason, to commit a crime, that, by itself, is not sufficient to convict him. "It is said that motive does not matter, but motive may be very material when it is sought to justify what until justified is a wrong." 279 U.S. 435, 537 (1929).

MUNICIPAL LAW

The law of a city, or, in international law, the law of a state as opposed to international law.

MUTUALITY OF OBLIGATION

Basically but not exhaustively, it means that in a contract both parties must be bound to its terms or neither is bound to its terms.

N

NATIONALITY

One speaks of the nationality of a person or a ship or an airplane as being Russian, American, etc.

NEGLIGENCE

"Actionable negligence consists of the neglect of the use of ordinary care or skill towards a person to whom the defendant owes a duty of observing ordinary care or skill, by which neglect the plaintiff without contributory negligence on his part, has suffered injury to his person or property." 11 Queens Bench Div. 503 (1883).

NEGOTIABLE INSTRUMENTS

Under the Uniform Commercial Code, a negotiable instrument must be signed by the maker or drawer, contain an unconditional promise to pay a sum certain in money, be payable on demand to order or to bearer. A check is probably the best example of a negotiable instrument although it can be made non-negotiable.

NEUTRALITY

In World War II, Sweden was a neutral nation, carefully avoiding censure of one of the warring parties by avoiding partiality.

NOLO CONTENDERE

A plea, usually as a result of a conference between counsel for the defendant and the prosecution, that the defendant will not defend himself. When the plea is accepted by the court, it has the effect, if not the stigma, of a plea of guilty.

NOMINAL DAMAGES

In a civil action, where the jury feels that defendant had committed a legal wrong, but one not worthy of substantial damages, it will award an insignificant sum in damages far less than that asked for by the plaintiff. In some instances, usually in cases of defamation, the award is so slight as to be a moral victory for the defendant.

NOTARY PUBLIC

"A notary public is a public, but not a state or governmental, official who has the power to take acknowledgements and affidavits, to administer oaths, to certify to the authenticity of documents, to take depositions of witnesses, and to protest commercial paper." Greene, *Law of Notaries Public* (Legal Almanac Series No. 14, 1955).

O

OBJECT

See EXCEPTION.

OBSCENITY

"Whether the tendency of the matter charged as obscenity is to deprave and corrupt those whose minds are open to such immoral influences, and into whose hands a publication of this sort may fall." 3 Queens Bench 360, 371 (1868). All attitudes towards obscenity, in a legal sense, seem to have sprung from this definition, although the courts today seem to operate on the principle that no one was ever seduced by a book.

OFFER

See CONTRACT.

OMBUDSMEN

A Scandinavian innovation to control the controllers. The ombudsman receives complaints from citizens about maladministrations of government officials, investigates the complaints, attempts to right any wrongs and can prosecute the wrongdoing officials. It has recently been adopted in Great Britain and is being considered by many of the United States.

OPINION

In common usage, it is used interchangeably with the decision or judgment of a court, but it should refer specifically to the formal and written statement of the court to be found in the reports of the various state and federal courts. The opinion of the court is the one that binds the parties to the litigation and from which precedents evolve. It is much easier to determine who won a case than what it stands for.

There are also concurring opinions, whereby a judge agrees as to who should win the case but differs as to the reasoning; and dissenting opinions, which, except in unusual circumstances, are usually flights of painful oratory, nostalgic glances to a world that never was or a member of the court riding his hobby horse. See PER CURIAM.

OPTION

The usual situation is where a person is interested in purchasing anything from stock to a home to a diamond ring and is given a specified amount of time to make up his mind. The sum usually requested to make sure the buyer is serious often becomes the down payment.

ORDINANCE

An ordinance is to a city what a law is to a state.

P

PAR VALUE

The face value of stock which may or may not be what it would cost to purchase it on the open market.

PAROL

The parol evidence rule does not permit a witness to vary the words of a written agreement. Parol evidence is spoken evidence.

PAROLE

A release from jail having the effect of cutting down on the parolee's sentence. It is usually granted for good behavior but the parole can be suspended, and the parolee returned to jail, for bad behavior. Probation, on the other hand, is where a person is convicted of a crime but, rather than sent to jail, is given a suspended sentence, and allowed to return to the community under supervision. Misbehavior can revive the sentence and result in incarceration for the probationer.

PARTNERSHIP

A business owned by two or more persons all of whom share in its profits and losses. It differs from a corporation in that the partners' personal assets can be liable for losses of the business.

A silent partner is one who has the same advantages and obligations of his associate or associates but prefers anonymity. The Uniform Partnership Act defines a partnership as "an association of two or more persons to carry on as co-owners of a business for profit." Although partnerships are not taxed as such, the Internal Revenue Bureau conveniently provides a form (Form 1065) for the listing of income derived from such a business venture.

PATENT

A grant made by law for a specific period of time so that the inventor may have the exclusive use of the product of his creativity.

PENALTY

See TAXATION.

PER CURIAM

An opinion representing the entire court and not associated with any specific judge. *Per curiam* opinions determine the issues between the litigating parties, usually without a reasoned opinion, and have been much criticized. A *per curiam* opinion has the psychological effect of showing the unanimity of the court. It should be distinguished from the expression "certiorari denied," which means that the court, without prejudice, refuses to consider the case and leaves the decision of the court below to stand. It should also be contrasted with a seriatim opinion, employed by English courts, where judges, each in turn, express their views.

PERCENTAGE DEPLETION

An unconscionable tax deduction allowed to those who exploit our natural resources for gain and profit.

PEREMPTORY CHALLENGE

In the selection of a jury each side can dismiss potential jurors peremptorily, i.e., for no apparent reason. Each side is limited in its number of peremptory challenges. A juror can always be dismissed for reason, that is, being related to a party to the litigation, accepting a bribe, etc.

PERJURY

A deliberate lie said under oath. An income tax form can be the basis of a government action for perjury against the signer.

PERPETUITY, RULE OF

The tendency of the law is not to let property be ruled from the grave and thus imposes limits on a testator in his disposition of property. The rule has been the subject of much recrimination by professors of law, much anguish for law students, and much recent legislation, credit or blame for which has been associated with Professor Leach of Harvard.

PERSONAL PROPERTY

Also called personalty. Anything that is not real property or realty.

PETIT JURY

Usually a body of twelve men or women selected from a larger panel to determine the facts (not the law although they have exercised the prerogative) in a trial at law.

PETITION

An application requesting relief from a court.

PLAINTIFF

The person for whom an action is brought is called the plaintiff. If plaintiff loses and appeals the case he becomes an appellant. If plaintiff wins, the defendant becomes the appellant. The party who has won the original case becomes the appellee in the appeal. A respondent, like an appellee, is the party against whom an appeal is brought. It is said that he who tries his own case has a fool for a client.

PLEADINGS

The technical means by which the parties to a litigation frame the issue which will be decided by the court. First there is the plaintiff's complaint or declaration and then the answer of the defendant.

PLEDGE

The use of personal property as security for a debt. The pledgor delivers the goods he wishes to pledge to the pledgee or creditor. When the debt is paid the property is returned, if not, the pledgee can sell it, under certain conditions, despite the fact he does not have title to the property pledged.

POLICE POWER

A convenient expression "to conciliate the mind to something that needs explanation: the fact that the constitutional requirement of compensation when property is taken cannot be pressed to its grammatical extreme; that property rights may be taken for public purposes without pay if you do not take too much; that some play must be allowed to the joints if the machine is to work. But police power often is used in a wide sense to cover and, as I said, to apologize for the general power of the legislature to make a part of the community uncomfortable by a change." 273 U.S. 418, 445-7 (1927). The usual defense against the police power, as in regulating wages, is that it violates the due process clause of the Constitution.

PREEMPT

Because both the federal government, and the states legislate on similar matters, such as labor, it is difficult to determine the areas within which each can operate. "When, as in this matter, the Constitution takes from the States only a portion of their otherwise absolute control, there may be expected difficulties in drawing the dividing line, because where it shall be put is a question of more or less. The trouble is inherent in the situation, but it is the same in kind that meets us everywhere else in the law. The question is whether the state law creates a direct burden upon what it is for Congress to control, and the facts of the specific case must be weighed." 219 U.S. 128, 138 (1911).

PREPONDERANCE OF EVIDENCE

A frequently used term by a judge in charging a jury. It is that intangible something extra that satisfies the jury that a party having the burden to prove its contention has done so.

PRICE DISCRIMINATION

The illegal efforts of a buyer or seller to gain a competitive price advantage. The purpose of the Robinson-Patman Act is to prevent the concentration of economic power and there are those who suspect it has not achieved its goal.

PRINCIPAL

The most commonly known type of principal is the one that sponsors an agent. See AGENT.

PRIVACY, RIGHT TO

Somewhat in the nature of a LIBEL, this tort action is designed to protect an individual from unwarranted publicity. See Gross, *Privacy* (Legal Almanac Series No. 54, 1964).

PROBATE

The vast number of wills create little stir and are simply filed with the probate court, their directions followed by a scrupulous executor, and their contents become a public record. Wills are also contested in the probate court and in some instances are recorded there prior to the death of the testator. Probate courts also handle such family matters as guardianship and adoption.

PROCEDURE

The rules which must be followed, within reason, so that law can be administered with some degree of prediction dictated by experience. The Federal Rules of Civil and Criminal Procedure have been adopted by many states as a sensible adjustment to the operation of the courts and the protection of the litigants. Many of the definitions in this dictionary define procedural rules.

PROCLAMATION

A much abused type of public notice of the President, a Governor or a Mayor announcing everything from National Pickle Week to Thanksgiving.

PROMISSORY NOTE

A negotiable instrument involving the maker of the note and the payee, to whom the money is owed. See also CHECK and NEGOTIABLE INSTRUMENTS.

PROPERTY

"The notion of property starts, I suppose, from confirmed possession of a tangible object and consists in the right to exclude others from interference with the more or less free doing with it as one wills." 209 U.S. 1, 19 (1908).

PROSECUTE

The function of the prosecuting attorney of the state or federal government is to conduct the trial against a defendant formally accused of a crime.

PROVISO

A condition, limitation or stipulation in a statute or in an agreement.

PROXIMATE CAUSE

A key issue in many negligence actions is whether the act of the defendant was the proximate cause of the injury to the plaintiff. There are many guidelines and definitions none of which have proved too satisfactory.

PUNITIVE DAMAGES

See DAMAGES

Q

QUASH

To quash an indictment is to render it void. It is not RES JUDICATA and a new indictment can be drawn curing the defects of the previous one.

QUITCLAIM

A deed wherein the grantor transfers to the grantee whatever claim of title he has in the land. See CONVEYANCE and DEED.

R

RATIFY

To approve, sanction and give full validity to a transaction. After the Revolution, our colonies ratified the Constitution.

REAL PROPERTY OR REALTY

A term most often applied to land and the things attached to the land. Callahan, *The Law of Real Estate* (Legal Almanac Series No. 4, 1960).

REBUT

To contradict. See PRIMA FACIE.

RECEIVER

A Receiver in Bankruptcy is one appointed by the court to supervise and act for the bankrupt's property.

RECOUPMENT

Recoup, counter claim and set-off are efforts of the defendant to reduce any damages should the plaintiff win his case.

REDEEM

When the debtor or pledgor satisfies the debt for which he gave security, the mortgagee or pledgee must return the personal property or release the mortgage which he holds.

REFEREE

A Referee in Bankruptcy hears all parties concerned with the future of the bankrupt's assets and decides what the best disposition would be with the court's permission.

REFERENDUM

A method of giving the people an opportunity to express their wishes by ballot on a specific legislative proposal.

REGULATIONS

In order to carry out the intent of the law, the various governmental departments issue regulations. They are the work of a government agency and not a legislature and therefore do not have the effect of law. The United States Government prints their regulations first in the *Federal Register*, which is published five times a week, and this information is arranged by topic in the *Code of Federal Regulations*.

REMAND

To return a case back from whence it came usually with orders by the higher court to proceed with the case in a particular manner. It is in effect a reversal of a lower court.

REPLY

In PLEADINGS there is the complaint of the plaintiff, the answer of the defendant and the reply of the plaintiff.

RESCIND

The rescission of a contract means to avoid or cancel or abrogate or annul a contract. To rescind is not necessarily to breach.

RESIDENCE

A bona fide residence is not necesarily the same as DOMICILE. One can consider Boston, Mass. a domicile, as he intends to return there, visit London for weeks on a business trip without it being either a domicile or residence, but have permanent quarters in Zurich sufficient for you to be adjudged a resident. If one is a resident of a foreign country, he can claim an income tax exemption by filing Form 2555.

RESPONDENT

See PLAINTIFF.

RESTATEMENT

The Restatement is an attempt by scholars and eminent practitioners to, in effect, codify the common law. Volumes have been published on torts, contracts, property and other topics. While courts are not obliged to follow the Restatement, they are persuasive enough to be frequently cited by courts in support of their reasoning.

RESTITUTION

An equitable remedy, usually preceded by the breaching or rescission of a contract, whereby the court attempts to restore both parties to where they were before the contract was made.

RETROACTIVE

To make something effective as of a prior time. In labor agreements, salary agreements are usually made retroactive to when the bargaining began rather than as of the time when the agreement was made. One of the problems in *Mapp v. Ohio* 367 U.S. 643 (1961) was whether the Supreme Court would consider its ruling, regarding state convictions based upon unconstitutionally obtained evidence, retroactive and thus result in many prisoners seeking release from jail.

REVERSED

Let us say that a Supreme Court of New York State, a trial court, decides a case for A. B appeals to the Appellate Division which reverses and decides for B. A carries the case to the highest court in New York, The Court of Appeals, which reverses and decides for A. If the situation is one that can be carried to the federal level, a final determination can be had from the United States Supreme Court.

RIGHTS

"All rights are intangible personal relations between the subject and the object of them created by law." 257 U.S. 99, 110 (1921).

RIPARIAN RIGHTS

With the advent of water recreation, the rights of owners of land on the banks of the water to use and not abuse their natural advantage has become increasingly significant. As in most law, what is abuse is a matter of degree, custom and regulation. The dominant servitude is the fellow upstream who can be enjoined from polluting the waters heading downstream. There is a growing awareness of public water rights protecting the week-end boatman and the city dwelling fisherman from having his favorite water spot desecrated.

ROE, RICHARD

Like John Roe, a wholly fictitious person, made necesary by the peculiarities of the old English action of ejectment.

S

SALE

The passing of title from the seller to the buyer for a price.

SANCTION

In present international law, it is an effort by economic means, public denunciation and United Nations action to insist that an outcast nation mend its way. In the year 1965, Rhodesia was a case in point.

SATISFACTION

To fulfill a legal obligation such as paying a judgment of the court.

SCIENTER

In some torts there must be knowledge on the part of a defendant to provoke liability such as knowingly harboring a vicious dog. This should be distinguished from *mens rea*, a term involving the intent of one to do a criminal act. In recent years, absolute liability has been replacing *mens rea* as a criminal law concept to the consternation of many professors. See 1964 *Annual Survey of American Law* 39.

SCINTILLA

If there is so much as a spark of evidence in a case, some courts permit it to go to a jury. Many states have abolished the rule.

SECURITIES

The technical meaning of a security is a pledge for payment of a debt. The Securities and Exchange Commission of the Federal Government is designed to protect the consumer in the issuance of notes, stocks, bonds, etc.

SECURITY

The guaranty that a creditor will be repaid. It may be a mortgage, personal property or a signature guaranteeing a debtor's credit.

SELF DEFENSE

The right to defend one's self as warranted by the circumstances. "Detached reflection cannot be demanded in the presence of an uplifted knife." 256 U.S. 335, 343 (1921).

SENTENCE

After a judgment of guilty, it is the formal pronouncement of the court which may be probation, a fine or a jail sentence. The limits of a sentence are determined by statute.

SEPARATE BUT EQUAL

The ignominious doctrine of Plessy v. Ferguson, 163 U.S. 537 (1896) that it was a feasible and constitutional classification, for purposes of transportation accommodations, for a state to segregate the races.

SEPARATION OF POWERS

See JUDICIARY.

SET-OFF

See RECOUPMENT.

SEXUAL OFFENSES

Usually described as offenses against morality and decency, they are set out in the penal code of each state and elaborated on by many court decisions. They include such crimes as prostitution, rape, incest, adultery, etc. Mueller, *Legal Regulation of Sexual Conduct* (Legal Almanac Series No. 9, 1961).

SHELLEY'S CASE

A court made rule designed to protect feudal rights. A leaves land to B, and, after B's death, to the heirs of B. The Rule in Shelley's case gives a fee simple (or ownership of the land) to B, and the children of B get nothing. The Rule has been abolished in most American jurisdictions. The story goes that a law professor asked a student, "What is the Rule in Shelley's Case;" and the student answered, "It's the same for him as for anybody else."

SITUS

Usually means the actual location of a piece of land.

SLANDER

Harmful oral statements in which the action lies in tort. See LIBEL.

SOVEREIGN IMMUNITY

A theory that has been much weakened in recent years particularly with regard to the right of a sovereign (The United States, a state, etc.) not to be sued in tort. The old theory holds that "A sovereign is exempt from suit, not because of any formal conception or obsolete theory, but on the logical and practical ground that there can be no legal right as against the authority that makes the law on which the right depends." 205 U.S. 349, 353 (1907)

SPECIFIC PERFORMANCE

Where money damages would not be adequate, a petitioner may request the court to grant him that which he bargained for whether it be a deed to land or a work of art. It is a proceeding in equity and courts are reluctant to grant it.

STATES' RIGHTS

A shibboleth used by the wrong people for the wrong purposes at the wrong time. Its dangerous aspect is that it suggests a state can defy Federal law by the will of its ruling cliches; its beneficial aspects is that large areas of self determination exist such as economic conditions and education.

STATUS OF FORCES AGREEMENT

The legal status of the armed forces of each member nation to the agreement when stationed on the territory of another member nation. It sets forth the rights, privileges, and responsibilities of visiting forces, and of individual members of such forces, including civilian employees of the Armed Forces and dependents of both groups.

STATUTE

See BILL. State laws are generally called Session Laws (occasionally Acts and Resolves); while federal laws are called Public Laws such as: *Public Law* 89-110 which is the *Voting Rights Act* of 1965 and which can be found in 79 *Statutes at Large* 437 (1965), the latter being the official and preferred citation.

STATUTE OF FRAUDS

Many transactions and sales cannot be enforced unless they are in writing and signed by the owner of the property (usually referred to as the party to be charged). The usual situation is a sale involving land. The original of this concept dates back to an English statute passed in 1678.

STATUTE OF LIMITATION

If causes of actions were allowed to run indefinitely, a party could wait twenty years before suing for a dog bite. Witnesses die, memories fade, customs change and so the law limits the right to bring an action to a fixed term. The limitations vary as to the type of action, and each state varies as to length, bringing about much uncertainty when one wishes to sue in state A, where there is time, for an action that took place in state B, where time has run out.

STAY

A postponement of an order of a court such as a stay of execution providing counsel for the defendant an opportunity to seek some relief which the normal course of the law had not provided.

STIPULATION

An agreement by opposing counsel as to the conduct of a trial.

SUBORNATION OF PERJURY

To procure or induce one to commit PERJURY.

SUBPOENA

An order requiring one to appear in court as a witness under penalty of law and usually providing something in the way of expenses.

SUBROGATION

A typical example of subrogation is where an insurance company agrees to pay any damages to its insured such as in liability insurance policies. The insurance company succeeds to any claims its insured may have against the party that is responsible for the damages. Where a party is substituted for another in a claim against a third party you can have subrogation.

SUBSIDIARY

Where one company, by owning a majority of shares of another company, controls it.

SUIT

"To maintain a suit is to uphold, continue on foot and keep from collapse a suit already begun." 275 U.S. 56, 61 (1927).

SUMMONS

The initiation of a suit against a defendant.

SUPREME COURT

The United States Supreme Court is the highest court in the land. The Supreme Court of New York is a trial court; the highest court of New York is the Court of Appeals. The court below the United States Supreme Court is the Court of Appeals. It is not the name of the court that gives it power, but its constitutional grant.

SURETY

One who promises to make good for the debt of another. The surety will stand in place of the debtor to the creditor.

SURROGATE

The name given in some states to the judge who has administration of probate matters.

SURVIVORSHIP

One is not an heir until he survives a testator.

T

TAX COURT

The United States Tax Court is a circuit court
that reviews the decisions of the Commissioner
of Internal Revenue and is in turn review-
able by the United States Courts of Appeal. One
of the anomalies of this situation is that an opinion of the Tax Court can be affirmed in one
Court of Appeals (See CIRCUIT COURT) and
reversed in another. This situation is one that
taxes the imagination.

TAXABLE INCOME

The taxpayer, after listing GROSS INCOME,
is permitted deductions, which, when subtracted
provide the figure upon which you must com-
pute your tax. Line 11d on the 1965 Form 1040
is where you list your taxable income.

TAXATION

". . . every exaction of money for an act is a dis-
couragement to the extent of the payment required, but that which in its immediacy is a dis-
couragement may be part of an encouragement
when seen in its organic connection with the
whole. Taxes are what we pay for civilized society, . . . A penalty on the other hand is intended altogether to prevent the thing
punished." 275 U.S. 87, 100 (1927). Goldberg,

Tax Planning for Today and Tomorrow (Legal Almanac Series No. 51, 1961).

TENANT

See LANDLORD AND TENANT.

TENDER

This term is technically defined in the Uniform Commercial Code. It has to do with the delivery of money or goods according to an agreement and obligating the other party to fulfill his part of the agreement.

TERM

A term of the United States Supreme Court begins the first Monday in October annually. For example, the October 1958 term covered opinions printed in volumes 358-360 of the United States Supreme Court. Decision day is the day, which used to be solely on Monday, that the Court announces what opinions it has decided. State courts have similar practices.

TESTAMENTARY

A testamentary disposition is nothing more than the contents of a will.

TESTATOR (male)

TESTATRIX (female)

The deceased who leaves a will.

TESTIFY

A person who gives evidence under oath, usually the witness at a trial.

TORT

"When a man commits a tort he incurs by force of the law a liability to damages, measured by certain rules. When a man makes a contract he incurs by force of the law a liability to damages, unless a certain promised event comes to pass." 190 U.S. 540, 543 (1903). Examples of torts are negligence, false imprisonment, malpractice, malicious prosecution and many other unrelated acts brought under one heading because they involve injury, and are distinguished from contract and crime, although, in some instances, they could come under that heading to achieve different purposes. See Francis, *Protection Through the Law* (Legal Almanac Series No. 55, 1964).

TREATY

An agreement between two or more nations.

TRIAL

Proceedings in court, civil and criminal, involving the parties to the litigation, a judge, and usually a jury.

TRUST

Trusts can be created by a living person or by a testator. They postpone the date of alienation, that is, title does not pass to the one benefiting from the trust, if at all, until a date set by the trustor or settlor or, if necessary, by the courts. It is a favorite device of tax lawyers to make a mockery of income and estate tax laws; and of cautious parents who prefer seeing their lifetime earnings spent by their heirs more in the fashion of a leaky faucet than a waterfall.

TYING ARRANGEMENTS

In antitrust law, the illegal attempt of a seller to condition the sale of one product on the buyer buying another product. Thus if A has a monopoly on wigs and conditions their sale on retailers buying dandruff remover with each wig, he may run afoul of the antitrust laws.

U

UNIFORM COMMERCIAL CODE

It is essential to business that there be uniform and predictable practices. The American Law Institute and the National Conference of Commissioners on Uniform State Laws, after many conferences and drafts prepared by outstanding authorities, drew up a Uniform Commercial Code which has been adopted, in varying degrees, by most of the commercial states of our nation as well as many of the others. It has proved a boon to the commercial world and to many publishers of law books.

UNIFORM STATE LAWS

Although our states follow the common law almost exclusively, they have realized that in some areas there must be uniform laws so that reciprocity is possible, such as the Uniform Reciprocal Enforcement of Support Act which will follow a defaulting husband all over the United States. There are many other uniform laws, particularly with regard to commercial matters, and there will be many more.

UNILATERAL

An example of a unilateral contract is this one found in *Corbin* on *Contracts*: "If A sends a book to B, offering to sell it at a price, and B keeps the book, either expressly or impliedly promising to pay the price, a contract is consummated by B's acceptance." This instance occurred in 158 Mass. 194 (1893).

USE

Our present day trust had its origin in the use. The Statute of Uses, 1535, attempted to abolish the alienation of land, and its failure was democracy's gain and feudalism's loss. For the types of uses see the June 1961 issue of the Harvard Law School Bulletin.

V

VENDEE

The buyer in a sale.

VENDOR

The seller in a sale.

VENUE

"Venue in its modern and municipal sense relates to and defines the particular county or territorial area within the state or district in which the cause or prosecution must be brought or tried. It commonly has to do with geographical subdivisions, relates to practice or procedure, may be waived, and does not refer to jurisdiction at all." 237 Mass. 482 (1921).

VERDICT

The decision of the jury.

VERTICAL MERGERS

As opposed to HORIZONTAL MERGER, a vertical merger is where a corporation or individual attempts to control the supply of his product, such as an aluminum fabricating company buying up its supplier of ingots; or theo utlets for his product, such as a manufacturer buying up a chain of retail stores that deal in his product.

VEST

The usual expression is that "title vests in A," which means that he is now the owner.

VOID

Many legal transactions are void because they did not comply with the law. A void marriage can result from two cousins marrying. A void contract was never a contract; but a voidable contract is one that the court will permit unless a party comes forth and asks the court to void it. A contract with an infant is one that is voidable.

VOTING RIGHTS ACT OF 1965

This federal act suspends discriminatory literacy tests, provides for registration by Federal examiners, directs the United States Attorney General to bring suit where a poll tax is found to be discriminatory and protects qualified persons seeking to vote and those aiding others to vote.

VACATE

To vacate a judgment is to set it aside or make it void; to vacate the premises is to move out of your apartment without intention of returning.

W

WAIVER

The relinguishment of a right. If you permit the statute of limitations to run on an action you could have against a party, you have waived your rights.

WARRANTY, BREACH OF

A breach of warranty occurs where a product is not what its maker or manufacturer states it to be. A large body of law has grown in this area making it unmanageable for a concise definition.

WILL

A document, advisedly prepared by an attorney, providing for the disposition of one's property after one's death. To die INTESTATE means that the deceased's property will pass to the heirs, or possibly be given to the state (escheat), according to law. See PROBATE. Callahan, *How To Make A Will Simplified* (Legal Almanac Series No. 2, 1961).

WRIT

The Great Writ, of course, is the writ of *Habeas Corpus*. This writ tests the lawfulness of detention. There is also the *Writ of Error Coram Nobis* which reviews and corrects errors of fact which were not known at the time of trial, and, which,

if known, would have resulted in a different out-
come.

WRONGFUL DEATH

At common law there was no cause of action if
the injured party was killed. To correct this every
state has a Lord Campbell's Act (it was an English law first) to provide redress for the family
of the deceased who has been negligently de-
stroyed.

APPENDIX

BRADLEY, Joseph P. (1813-1892).
The right to follow any of the common occupations of life is an inalienable right, . . . *111 U.S. 746, 762 (1884).*

It may be that it is the obnoxious thing in its mildest and least repulsive form; but illegitimate and unconstitutional practices get their first footing in that way, namely, by silent approaches and slight deviations from legal modes of procedure. This can only be obviated by adhering to the rule that constitutional provisions for the security of person and property should be liberally construed. *116 U.S. 616, 635 (1886).*

BREWER, David J. (1837-1910).
The paternal theory of government is to me odious. The utmost possible liberty to the individual, and the fullest possible protection to him and his property is both the limitation and duty of government. *143 U.S. 517, 551 (1892).*

Constitutional provisions do not change, but their operation extends to new matters, as the modes of business and the habits of life of the people vary with each succeeding generation. *158 U.S. 564, 591 (1895).*

[The Declaration of Independence] is the thought and the spirit, and it is always safe to read the letter of the Constitution in the spirit of the Declaration of Independence. *165 U.S. 150, 160 (1897).*

BUTLER, Pierce. (1866-1939).
It has always been recognized in this country, and it is well to remember, that few if any of the rights of the people guarded by fundamental law are of greater importance to their happiness and safety than the right to be exempt from all unauthorized, arbitrary or unreasonable inquiries and disclosures in respect of their personal and private affairs. *279 U.S. 263, 292 (1929).*

Freedom of contract is the general rule and restraint the exception. *287 U.S. 283, 288 (1932).*

CHOATE, Joseph H. (1832-1917).
The Act of Congress (the income tax law) which we are

impugning before you is communistic in its purposes and tendencies, and is defended here upon principles as communistic, socialistic—what shall I call them—populistic as ever have been addressed to any political assembly in the world. . . . I have thought that one of the fundamental objects of all civilized government was the preservation of the rights of private property. *157 U.S. 429, 532, 534 (1895).*

DELOLME, Jean L. (1740-1806).

. . . it is a fundamental principle with the English lawyers, that parliament can do every thing, *except* making a woman a man, or a man a woman. *The Constitution of England, 1853, page 102.*

DILLON, John F. (1831-1914).

But verily reform is a plant of slow growth in the sterile gardens of the practising and practical lawyer. *Laws and Jurisprudence of England and America, 1895, page 340.*

DOUGLAS, William O. (1898-   ).

It may be most desirable to give corporations this protection from the operation of legislative process. But that question is not for us. It is for the people. If they want corporations to be treated as humans are treated, if they want to grant corporations this large degree of emancipation from state regulation, they should say so. The Constitution provides a method by which they may do so. *337 U.S. 562, 581 (1949).*

FIELD, Stephen J. (1816-1899).

It would be a most singular result of a constitutional provision intended for the protection of every person against partial and discriminating legislation by the states, should cease to exert such protection the moment the person becomes a member of a corporation. We cannot accept such a conclusion. On the contrary, we think it well established . . . that whenever a provision of the Constitution . . . guaranties to persons the enjoyment of property, . . . or prohibits legislation . . . affecting it, . . . the court will always look beyond the name of the artificial being to the individuals whom it represents. *13 Fed. 722, 744 (1882).*

FRANK, Jerome. (1889-1957).

I want, therefore, to stress the fact that litigation in our courts is still a fight. The fighting, to be sure, occurs in a courtroom, and is supervised by a government officer known as a judge. Yet, for the most part, a law-suit remains a sort of subliminated, regulated brawl, a private battle conducted in a court-house. *Courts on Trial, 1949, page 7.*

HAND, Learned. (1872-1961).

I question whether in the end men will regard that as obscene which is honestly relevant to the adequate expression of innocent ideas, and whether they will not believe that truth and beauty are too precious to society at large to be mutilated in the interests of those most likely to pervert them to base *uses. 209 Fed. 119, 120, 121 (1913).*

Words are not only the keys of persuasion, but the triggers of action, and those which have no purport but to counsel the violation of law cannot by any latitude of interpretation be a part of that public opinion which is the final source of government in a democratic state. *244 Fed. 535, 540 (1917).*

. . . I must say that as a litigant, I should dread a lawsuit beyond almost anything else short of sickness and of death. *3 Lectures on Legal Topics, 1926, page 105.*

(A metaphor) is ordinarily a symptom of confused thinking. *31 F. 2d 265, 267 (1929).*

. . . The verdict of the jury is not the conclusion of a syllogism of which they are to find only the minor premiss, but really a small bit of legislation ad hoc, like the standard of care. *83 F. 2d 156, 157 (1936).*

. . . the interest protected by the First Amendment; . . . it presupposes that right conclusions are more likely to be gathered out of a multitude of tongues, than through any kind of authoritative selection. To many this is, and always will be, folly; but we have staked upon it our all. *52 F. Supp. 362, 372 (1943).*

It is possible, because of its indirect social or moral effect, to prefer a system of small producers, each dependent for his success upon his own skill and character, to one in which the great mass of those engaged must accept the direction of a few. *148 F. 2d 416, 427 (1945).*

[The words of the income tax act] dance before my eyes in a meaningless procession: cross-reference to cross-reference, exception upon exception—couched in abstract terms that offer no handle to seize hold of . . . *57 Yale Law Journal 167, 169 (1947).*

HUGHES, Charles E. (1862-1948).

. . . freedom of contract is a qualified and not an absolute right. There is no absolute freedom to do as one wills or to contract as one chooses. . . . Liberty implies the absence of arbitrary restraint, not immunity from reasonable regulations and prohibitions imposed in the interests of the community. *219 U.S. 549, 567 (1911).*

A dissent in a court of last resort is an appeal to the brooding spirit of the law, to the intelligence of a future day, when a later decision may possibly correct the error in which the dissenting judge believes the court to have been betrayed. *The Supreme Court of the United States, 1928, pages 67, 68.*

The vast expansion of this field of administrative regulation in response to the pressure of social needs is made possible under our system by adherence to the basic principles that the legislature shall appropriately determine the standards of administrative action and that in administrative proceedings of a quasi-judicial character the liberty and property of the citizen shall be protected by the rudimentary requirements of fair play. *304 U.S. 1, 14 (1938).*

MAGRUDER, Calvert. (1893-   ).

The power of a sonorous phrase to command uncritical acceptance has often been encountered in the law . . . the view (suggesting illicit intercourse to a female resulting in mental disturbance) being, apparently, that there is no harm in asking." *49 Harvard Law Reveiw 1033, 1055 (1936).*

The position of a judge has been likened to that of an oyster—anchored in one place, unable to take the initiative, unable to go out after things, restricted to working on and digesting what the fortuitous eddies and currents of litigation may wash his way. *55 Harvard Law Review 193, 194 (1941).*

MAXWELL, Haymond. (?).

God's noblest creation is a good woman. Her virtue is at the summit of human attributes. *106 W. Va. 446, 455, 456; 145 S.E. 813 (1928).*

McREYNOLDS, James C. (1862-1946).

And while "an overspeaking judge is no well-tuned cymbal," neither is an amorphous dummy, unspotted by human emotions, a becoming receptacle for judicial powers. *255 U.S. 22, 43 (1921).*

95

MURPHY, Frank. (1890-1949).

The power of the licensor against which John Milton directed his assault by his "Appeal for the Liberty of Unlicensed Printing" is pernicious not merely by reason of the censure of particular comments but by reason of the threat to censure comments on matters of public concern. It is not merely the sporadic abuse of power by the censor but the pervasive threat inherent in its very existence that constitutes the danger to freedom of discussion. *310 U.S. 88, 97 (1940)*.

If this Court is to err in evaluating claims that freedom of speech, freedom of the press, and freedom of religion have been invaded, far better than it err in being overprotective of these precious rights. *316 U.S. 584, 623 (1942)*.

PARSONS, Theophilus. (1797-1882).

It is dangerous to attempt being wiser than the law. *5 Mass. 547, 557 (1809)*.

PAUL, Randolph E. (1890-1956).

. . . every signpost points to increased and increasing taxes. Taxpayers may in a few years look back at the Revenue Act of 1940 with the nostalgia of taxpayers remembering in 1918 to happy days of 1916. *Studies in Federal Taxation, Third Series, 1940, page vi*.

PEGLER, Westbrook. (1894-   ).

[A court] is just a room where people commit perjury and lawyers outsmart one another at the expense of individual chumps who get pinched or sued. *Boston American, July 15, 1957*.

PHILLIPS, Wendell. (1811-1884).

(Rufus Choate) who made it safe to murder, and of whose health thieves asked before they began to steal. *See Fuess, Rufus Choate, 1928, page 141*.

POWELL, Thomas R. (1880-1955).

. . . cases get distinguished and distinguished till they provoke the aphorism that a distinguished case is a case that is no longer distinguished. *53 Harvard Law Review 529, 537 (1940)*.

RUTLEDGE, Wiley. (1894-1949).

Precedent is not all-controlling in law. There must be room for growth, since every precedent has an origin. But it is the essence of our tradition for judges, when they stand at the end of a marked way, to go forward with caution keeping sight, so far as they are able, upon the great landmarks left behind and the direction they point ahead. *327 U.S. 1, 43 (1946).*

SEABURY, Samuel. (1873-1958).

As we look at some of the uses which the criminal classes have made of constitutional provisions, one might suppose that the farseeing barons who wrung the Great Charter from King John at Runnymede were intent upon safeguarding the twentieth century racketeer, gangster, kidnapper, gunman and corrupt political leader in the prosecution of the sinister vocations. It ought to be possible to find a way, by judicial interpretation, to use these constitutional provisions for the protection of liberty without giving them such fanciful and far-fetched interpretations as to convert them into a weapon by which criminals can make war safely upon organized society and its law-abiding members. *18 American Bar Association Journal 371 (1932).*

SHAW, George B. (1856-1950).

The way to get to the merits of a case is not to listen to the fool who imagines himself impartial, but to get it argued with reckless bias for and against. *See Times Literary Supplement, May 20, 1960, page 316.*

STORY, Joseph. (1779-1845).

The perfect lawyer, like the perfect orator, must accomplish himself for his duties by familiarity with every study. It may truly be said, that to him nothing, that concerns human nature or human art, is indifferent and useless. He should search the human heart, and explore to their sources the passions, and appetites, and feelings of mankind. *Miscellaneous Writings, 1852, page 527.*

VEBLEN, Thorstein B. (1857-1929).

The lawyer is exclusively occupied with the details of predatory fraud, . . . inchicane, . . . and success in the profession is therefore accepted as marking a large endowment of that barbarian astuteness which has always commanded man's respect and fear. *Theory of the Leisure Class, 1899, 231.*

WOOLSEY, John M. (1877-1945).

The value of a lawyer's services is not measured by time or labor merely. The practice of law is an art in which success depends as much as in any other art on the application of imagination—and sometimes inspiration—to the subject-matter. *37 F. 2d 749, 750 (1930).*

COMMON AND UNCOMMON LATIN LEGAL WORDS, TERMS AND PHRASES

A

AB ANTE
From before; beforehand.

AB EXTRA
From without; outside.

AB INTRA
From within.

ACTIO IN REM.
A real action.

AD ARBITRIUM
At pleasure; at will.

ADDENDA
Additions.

AD DIEM
At or to the day.

AD LIEM
For the suit.

AD VALOREM
According to the value.

A FORTIORI
By so much stronger reason; on the strongest side.

AMBIGUITAS LATENS
Latent ambiguity.

AMBIGUITAS PATENS
Patent ambiguity.

ANTE LITEM CONTESTATAM
Before the action is contested.

ANTE NUPTIAL
Before marriage.

A PRIORI
From the former.

ARGUENDO
In arguing; in the course of the argument.

ASSUMPSIT
He has promised.

B

BONA
Goods; property.

C

CAUSA CAUSANS
The efficient cause; the immediate cause.

CAUSAE JUSTAE
Legal grounds.

CAUSA MORTIS
In prospect of death.

CAUTIO PRO EXPENSIS
Security for costs.

CAVEAT EMPTOR
Let the buyer beware.

COGNOSCIT
He acknowledges; he confesses.

COMMUNE BONUM
A common good; a matter of mutual or general advantage.

COMMUNI CONSENSU
By common consent.

COMPENSANTO
Recompense; a set-off.

COMPONERE LITES
To settle disputes.

COMPOS MENTIS
Sound of mind; of sound mind.

CONFLICTUS LEGUM
A conflict of laws.

CONJURATIO
An oath.

CONSIDERATIO CURIAE
The judgment of the Court.

CONSTAT
It appears; a certificate of that which appears on the record.

CONTESTIO LITES
The disputing of a suit.

CONTRA
Against; on the contrary; otherwise.

CONTRA PACEM
Against the peace.

CONTRAPOSITO
A plea or answer.

CONVENTIO
An agreement or convenant.

COPIA VERA
A true copy of an official document.

CORPUS
Body; the capital fund as distinguished from the income.

CORPUS JURIS
The body of the law.

CRIMEN FALSI
The crime of forgery.

CRIMEN FURTI
The offense of theft.

CRIMEN INCENDI
The offense of arson.

CUI BONO?
To what good? To purpose?

What will be the better of it? What good will it do?

CUI MALO?
Whom will it harm?

CUJIUSDAM IGNOTE
Of some person unknown.

CULPA
An act of fault or neglect causing damage but not implying an intent to injure.

CULPA LATA
Gross negligence.

CUM
When; as; whereas; with.

CUM GRANO SALES
With a grain of salt; with an allowance for exaggeration.

CUM NOTA
With caution.

CUM ONERE
With the burden or incumbrance.

CURATOR BONIS
Guardian of the property.

CUSTODIA LEGIS
Custody of the law or the Court.

CY-PRES
As nearly as possible. Where the court cannot carry out the exact terms of a writing, it will, under certain circumstances, attempt to effecuate as nearly as possible the writer's true intention.

D

DAMNUM IN JURE
Damage in law. Loss or damage by injury or wrongful act.

DE
Of; concerning. This is the first word of many terms and phrases.

DE AUDITI
By hearsay.

DEBITUM
An act or forbearance to which a person is obliged. A debt.

DECISIS LITES
The settlement of a dispute; a composition.

DE COMPUTO
Of accounting.

DE DIE IN DEM
From day to day; continuously.

DE DONIS
Of gifts.

DE EXECUTIONE JUDICII
Of execution of judgment.

DEFENDERE UNICA MANU
To wage law; a denial of an accusation upon path.

DEFICIT
Something wanting.

DEFORTIATIO
A distress. A holding of goods for satisfaction of a debt.

DE FUTURO
Of or relating to the future.

DE GRATIA
As a favor.

DEHORS
Outside; without; foreign to.

DE INCREMENTO
Of increase.

DE INJURIA SUA PROPRIA
Of his own wrong.

DE INTEGRO
Afresh; anew.

DE JURIS FONTIBUS
Of the origin or source of law.

DELATOR
An accuser; an informer.

DELICTA PUBLICA
Public wrongs; crimes.

DEMORARI
To abide; to demur.

DE NOVO
Afresh; anew; over again; as a trial *de novo*.

DE QUESTU SUO
Of his own gain.

DE QUODAM IGNOTO
Of some person unknown.

DESIDERATUM
Anything wished for; a requisite.

DETINUIT
He has detained.

DE ULTERIORIBUS DAMNS
Of further damages.

DICTUM
An order; award; a saying or opinion of a judge.

DOLO POXIMA
Bordering on fraud.

DIMINIUM EMINENS
Eminent domain. The right which every state or sovereign power has to use the property of its citizens for the common welfare. The right is very basis of the right to taxation.

DONATIO
A donation; a gift.

DUCES TECUM
You shall bring with you, a writ commanding a person to produce in Court a document which may be in his possession.

DUODENA
A jury of 12 men.

DURANTE LITE
During the continuance of a suit.

DURANTE VITA
During life.

E

EAT INDE SINE DIE
That he go without a pay, *i.e.,* be dismissed without any further discontinuance or adjournment. The words used on the aquittal of a defendant.

EMPTOR
A buyer.

ESSE IN BONIS
To be in possession of a thing.

ESTOPPEL
To stop.

ET IDEO
And therefore.

ET SEQUITUR
And it follows. Abbr. *et seq.*

EX CATHEDRA
From the chair.

EX CONFESSO
By one's own profession.

EX CURIA
Out of Court.

EX DELICTO
EX MALEFICIO
From a fault or offense. From a tort.

EX PARTE
On one side only.

EX POST FACTO
From an after-act; after a deed is done.

EX RATIONE LEGIS
By reason of law.

EX TEMPORE
Without premeditation; without preparation; off-hand.

F

FACERE LEGEM
To make law.

FSCTUM PROBANS
The evidence which proves a thing.

FELLEO ANIMO
With a felonious intent.

FIAT JUSTITA
Let justice be done.

FORIS FACTUS
A forfeit.

G

GRADATIM
By degrees; by little and little; gradually.

GRATIS
For nothing; without reward.

GRAVE DELICTUM
A serious offense.

H

HABEAS CORPUS
That you have the body. The great remedy of law which provides for the violation of personal liberty, as by illegal imprisonment.

HABERE LICERE
To have permission.

HAECA VERBA
These words.

HOC EST
That is.

HOC PARATUS EST VERIFICARE
This he is ready to verify.

HOLOGRAPH
A deed written entirely by the grantor himself in his own hand.

I

IDEM PER IDEM
The same by the same; like by like. An illustration or proof which add nothing to the consideration of the question.

ID QUOD INTEREST
That which is of importance.

ILLICITE
Unlawfully.

IMPRIMATUR
Let it be printed.

IN ABSENTUM
In the absence.

IN ACTU
In the very act.

IN ALIO LOCO
In another place.

IN ANTIQUIOREM
In order of time.

IN ARBITRIUM JUDICIS
At the pleasure or discretion of the judge.

IN ARTICULO MORTIS
At the point of death; in a dying state.

IN BANCO
In bench. A judge sitting *in banco,* in court, not in chambers.

IN CAMERA
In private; in chambers. Hearing *in camera* means hearing a cause in chambers where reasons of a public nature (*e.g.,* evidence of a delicate or indecent character) suggest the propriety of such a course.

IN CAUSA
In the case.

INCERTUS DIES
Uncertain day.

INCIPITUR
It is begun; the beginning.

IN CURIA
In court.

IN CUSTODIA LEGIS
In the custody or keeping of the law.

INDEBITATUS ASSUMPSIT
Being indebted, he undertook; an action founded on an implied promise.

INDICIA
Signs; marks.

INDICTATUS
Indicted.

INDISTANTER
Forwith; without delay.

INDORSO
On the back.

IN ESSE
In being. Actually existing.

IN EXTENSO
From beginning to end, leaving out nothing; at length; fully; without abridgment.

IN EXTREMIS
In the last moments; on its last legs; in a shaky condition.

IN FACTO ET JURE
In fact and in law.

IN HOC STATUE
In the present state of matters.

IN IISDEM TERMINUS
In the same terms.

IN INITIO
In the beginning.

IN INFINITUM
To no end; without limit.

INJURIA CUM DAMNO
An injury or wrong accompanied with damage.

IN LOCO PARENTIS
In the place of a parent.

IN PARI DELICTO
In equal guilt. In like offense.

IN RE
In the matter of. Used in entitling matters other than actions, in which there is not any plaintiff or defendant. The words, when used at the beginning of a lawyer's letter, indicate the subject of the letter.

IN REM
To or against the property; to the point.

IN STATU QUO
In the condition in which he or it was before; in the former condition.

INTER VIVOS
Among the living. A gift or transfer inter vivos means a gift or transfer by a living person to a living person; as opposed to one by will.

IN TOTO
Totally; altogether; on the whole.

IN TRANSITU
During the passage; while in transit.

INTRA VIRES
Within its powers or jurisdiction. As opposed to *ultra vires*.

IPSE DIXIT
He himself said it. Used to denote an assertion resting on the authority of an individual.

IPSO FACTO
By the very fact itself.

J

JUS DOMICILII
The law of the domicile.

JUS ET SEISINAM
Right and possession.

L

LACHES
Negligence. Laches has been defined to be "a neglect to do some thing which by law a man is obliged to do."

LEGATUM
A bequest; legacy.

LEX FORI
The law of the place of the tribunal in which any case is tried.

LICENTIA
A license; a power or authority given to a person to do some lawful act.

LIS
A suit; action; dispute.

LIS MOTA
The dispute having arisen.

LIS PENDENS
A suit pending.

LITERATUM
Literally; letter for letter.

M

MALA FIDES
Bad faith, as opposed to *bona fides,* good faith.

MALA IN SE
Things evil in themselves.

MALO ANIMO
With an evil intent.

MISFEASANCE
A misdeed or trespass.

MODUS OPERANDI
The manner of operation or working. The way or mode of proceeding, or of setting to work.

MORTIS CAUSA
In prospect of death.

MOS PRO LEGE
Usage for law. Long established usage will stand in the place of law.

NIHIL. NIHILS
Nothing.

NIHIL DICIT
He says nothing.

NOMINE EXPENSARUM
In the name of expenses. In lieu of costs.

NON ALLEGATUM
Not pleaded.

NON COMPOS
Insane; incompetent.

NON CONSTAT
It does not appear. It is not evident.

NON DEBET
He owes not; he ought not.

NUL TORT
No wrong.

NUNC AUT NUNQUAM
Now or never.

NUNC PRO TUNC
Now for then; meaning that a judgment is entered, or document enrolled, so as to have the same legal force and effect as if it had been entered or enrolled on some earlier day on which it should have properly been done.

N

NE BAILA PAS
He has not delivered.

NE EXEAT
Let him not depart.

NIENT CULPABLE
Not guilty.

O

OBITER
Incidentally.

OBITER DICTUM
A saying by the way. An incidental opinion. A dictum of a judge on a point not directly relevant to the case before him.

OMNIA PLACITA
All pleas.

ONUS PROBANDI
The obligation or burden of proving; burden of proof.

OPERATUM FACTUM
Overt act. An open act which by law must be manifestly proved.

ORDO CURIAE
The order of the court.

ORE TENUS
By word of mouth; orally; verbally.

OYER ET TEMINER
To hear and determine.

OYEZ
Hear ye; pronounced by the criers of the United States Supreme Court. "O yea."

P

PACEATUR
Let him be freed or discharged.

PACTA CONVENTA
Conditions agreed upon.

PACTIO
A bargain or covenant.

PAIX
Peace.

PAR
Equal.

PARES
Equals; the peers or equals of the defendant.

PARI JURE
By equal right.

PARI RATIONE
For the same reason.

PAROL
By word or mouth; oral speech.

PASSIM
Everywhere; on every side; all through.

PECUNIA
Money.

PEINE
Penance; penalty.

PER ASSENSUM PARTIUM
With consent of the parties.

PER ATTORNATUM
By attorney.

PER CONTRA
On the other side; on the contrary.

PER CURIAM NON ALLOCATUR
It is not allowed by the court.

PER DAMNATIONEM
By condemnation.

PER DIEM
By the day; per day.

PER FAS
By that which is allowed or permitted; lawfully; in a lawful manner.

PER LAPSUM TEMPORIS
By lapse of time.

PER QUOD
By which; whereby.

PER SE
By itself. Alone. Where a person objects to an act *per se* he means that he would object to it under any circumstances whatever.

PERSONA DESIGNATA
A person described.

PER TESTES
By witness.

PER TAT
By so many.

PETITIO
Petition; court; declaration.

PETIT JUDICIUM
He seeks judgment.

PIA FRAUS
A friendly stratagem.

PIGNUS
A pledge of anything for money lent.

PLACET
It pleases. Decree; ordinance; official order.

PLENO JURE
With full authority.

POSITO
A claim; argument.

POST DIEM
After the day.

POST LITEM MOTAM
After the dispute arose. After a suit has been in contemplation.

POST NATUS
Born afterwards.

POST NUPTIAL
After marriage.

POST ORBIT
After death.

POSTULATIO
A complaint; an application for redress.

POTESTES ALIENANDI
Power to alienate; right of alienation.

PROEJUDICIA
Precedents.

PRAEMIUM
A reward; present; consideration.

PRAESUMPTIO JURIS
Presumption of law.

PRECARIO
Held by permission.

PRECLUDI NON
Not to be barred.

PRIMA FACIE
At first sight. On the first appearance. A party is said to have a *prima facie* case when the evidence in his favor is sufficiently strong for his opponent to be called on to answer it. Such evidence is called *prima facie* evidence, and can be overthrown only by the rebutting evidence adduced on the other side.

PRIMO
In the first class.

PRINCIPALE RECORDUM
The principal or original record.

PRINCIPIIS ABSTA
Nip in the bud; oppose beginning; meet the very beginning.

PRIOR PATENS
The first applicant. Used in probate practice.

PRIT
Ready.

PRIVATO CONSENSU
by one's own consent.

PRO
For; in respect of.

PROBATUM EST
It has been proved.

PROCEDENDO
In proceeding.

PRO CONFESSO
As confessed.

PRO ET TEMPORE
For place and time.

PRO NON SCRIPTO
As if not written or inserted.

PROPINQUI ET CONSANGUINEI
The nearest of kin.

PROPRIA MANU
With his own hand.

PROPTER AFFECTUM
By reason of bias or partiality.

PROPTER QUOD
On account of which thing, matter or circumstance.

PRO QUERENTE
For the plaintiff.

PRO TANTO
For so much; to that extent; as far as it will go.

PROTESTANDO
In protesting.

PROUT
According as; even as.

PRO VERITATE
As true.

PROVISO
Provided; stipulation; caution; condition. A condition inserted into a deed upon the observance whereof the validity of the deed depends.

PROXIMUS AMICUS
The next friend or next of kin.

PUBLICA JURIS
Of public right. A thing so-called when it is public property.

Q

QUA
In what; in which; in the character of; as far as; so far as regards.

QUAERE
Ask; inquire. A note for the reader to make further inquiry, where any point of law or matter of debate is doubted as most having sufficient authority to maintain it.

QUAM
As; which.

QUANDO
When.

QUANTUM
How much; proportion.

QUANTUM MERIT
So much as he deserved.

QUANTUM SUFFICIT
As much as is sufficient. A sufficient quantity.

QUARE
Wherefore; why.

QUASI
As if; as it were; in a manner.

QUASI DICAT
As if to say; abbrev. *q.d.*

QUENDAM
A certain one.

QUERENS
A plaintiff or complainant.

QUERITUR
He complains.

QUID
What.

QUIDEM
Indeed; truly.

QUID QUO PRO
One thing for another; an equivalent; a mutual exchange; *e.g.,* a mutual undertaking in a contract.

QUIETARE
To quit, acquit; or to discharge; to save harmless.

QUOD ULTRA
As to the rest.

QUOD ANIMO
With what intent.

QUODAMNADO
In some manner.

QUOD CIPIATUR
That he be taken.

QUOD CUM
That whereas. Used by way of recital.

QUOD EST
Which is. Abbrev. *q.e.*

QUOD FUIT CONCESSUM
Which was agreed to.

QUOD NON ETA EST
That is not so; which is not so.

QUOD VIDE
Which see. Used to refer a reader to the word, chapter, etc. referred to. Abbrev. *q.v.*

QUO JURE
By what right.

QUONDAM
At a certain time; at one time; once; formerly; former.

QUORUM
Of whom. Certain individuals among persons invested with any power, or with the exercise of any jurisdiction, without whom any number of the others cannot proceed to execute the power given by the commission. The *minimum* number of persons necessarily present, in order that business may be proceeded with at any meeting for the dispatch of business.

QUOTA
So many as; share; proportion.

QUO WARRANTO
By what authority.

R

RATIO
An account; a rule of proportion; reason.

RATIO LEGIS
The reason of the law.

RATIONALE
A statement of reasons. An exposition of the principles of a subject.

RATIONE DOMICILLI
By reason of domicile.

RE
In the nature of.

RECTATUS
Suspected or arraigned; accused.

RECTITUDO
Right of justice. A legal due, tribute, or payment.

RECTUM ROGARE
To ask for right. To petition the judge to do right.

REDEUNDO
In returning.

REMANENT
It remains; postponing a trial.

REPLEVIN
Relief.

RES
A word of the most general and extensive signification denoting anything that may be thought, done or spoken of. A thing; a something; a matter; affair; event; circumstances; case; an act; forbearance; a person; a right; an obligation.

RES GESTAE
The facts of a transaction. The gist of the thing. The material facts of a case, as opposed to mere hearsay. Things done or spoken in the course of a transaction of which proof may be received, as the words used at seditious meetings, to show the objects and character of such meetings.

RES INTEGRA
An entire thing. An affair not broached or meddled with. A point not covered by the authority of a decided case, so that a judge may decide it upon principle alone.

RES NOVA
Something new. A matter not yet decided.

RESPECTUS
Respite; delay; forbearance; continuation of time.

RESPONDEAT OUSTER
Let him answer over; *i.e.*, when a dilatory plea put in by the defendant has been overruled by the Court, let him put in a more substantial plea, or answer over in some better manner.

RESPONDEAT SUPERIOR
Let the principal answer. The general rule is, that the principal is civilly (and, in some cases, criminally) for the frauds, torts negligences, malfeasances and omissions of his agent, when done *in the course of his employment*, though not sanctioned, but even forbidden by the principal. The rule applies, *let the superior answer for it*, for he holds out his agent as competent, and so warrants his fidelity, skill, and good conduct in all matters within the scope of his agency. But if the act was not done in the course of his employment, but while the servant or agent was solely engaged upon *some purpose of his own*, or if the act was simply *wilful* or *malicious* on his part, or *beyond the scope of his authority*, express or implied, the master is not answerable. It is a question of fact whether a particular act is within the scope of the employment, though not in the ordinary course.

RES SINGULARES
Particular things.

RES UPSA LOQUITER
The thing speaks for itself. A is injured by a barrel falling out of B's window. No negligence can be proved against A. The Court holds that the circumstance speaks for itself and B is liable.

REUS
A defendant, a plaintiff. Strictly, any party to a case. A party to a stipulation.

S

SALVO JURE
Saving the right. Without prejudice to. An exception or reservation.

SANS CONTRACT
Without contract.

SATIS ACCIPERE
To take security or bail.

SATISFACTO
Satisfaction; compensation; amends; reparation.

SCIENDUM
To be known.

SCILICET
To wit. That is to say. Being understood. Abbrev., *Sc.*

SCUTUM
A shield.

SECTA
A suit. A witness or followers of a plaintiff.

SECUNDUM REGULAS
According to rules.

SECUS
Otherwise; contrariwise; not so.

SED NON ALLOCATUR
But it is not allowed.

SED VIDE
But see.

SEMBLE
It seems. Used in reports to show that a point is not decided

directly, but may be inferred. Abbrev., *Sem.* or *Semb.*

SEMEL ET SIMUL
At once and together.

SEMPER IDEM
Always the same.

SEMPER PARATUS
Always together.

SENU JURIDICO
In a judicial sense.

SEQUENDO
In following.

SERIATIM
Severally and in order; one by one; in a series; separately; individually.

SIC
So. Thus. In such a manner.

SECUT ALIAS
As at another time. A second writ sent out when the first was not executed.

SICAT ANTE
As before.

SIGILIUM
Seal; signature.

SIGNUM
A mark; sign.

SIMILITER
In like manner.

SINE DUBRO
Without a doubt.

SINE FACTO EJUS
Without any act on his part.

SINE SCRIPTIS
Without writing; unwritten.

SINE QUO NON
Without which nothing is to be done. An indispensible condition.

SI QUANDO
If when.

SITUS
Location; situation.

SOLIDATUM
Absolute right or property.

SALUTIO
A discharge; payment. The performance of that to which a person is bound.

SPONTA SUAE
Of one's own accord; unsolicited.

STARE DICISIS, ET NON MOVERE QUIETA
To stand by matters decided, and not to stir up points set at rest.

STATUS
Legal position.

STET
Let it stand.

SUB JUDICE
Under investigation or consideration.

SUB NOMINEE
Under the name of.

T

TAM QUAM
So as; as well as.

TARDE VENIT
It came too late.

TESTAMENTUM INJUSTUM
A void will.

TESTARI
To be witnessed.

TORT
Wrong or injury.

TOTUM
The whole; all; entire; as opposed to the *pars* (part).

TRANSGRESSIO
A trespass.

TRANSITUS
A transit; the passing from one place to another.

U

UBI
Where.

UBI SUPRA
Where above mentioned.

ULTRA
Beyond; further; additional.

ULTRA VIRES
Beyond authority; beyond power or jurisdiction.

ULTRA VIRES AB INITIO
Beyond power from the beginning.

UNO ANIMO
With one mind.

UNUM ET IDEM
One and the same.

UNUM ET IDEM
One and the same.

USANCE
Use; interest; usury.

USUS FORI
The practice or usage of courts.

V

VACUA POSSESSIO
Vacant possession *i.e.,* free and unburdened possession.

VALOR
Value or price of anything.

VENIRE
To come.

VENUE
The neighborhood from where the jury comes to try causes.

VERBIS OBLIGATIO
Verbal contract.

VERE DICTUM
A true statement; a verdict.

VERSUS
Against. Abbrev., *v.*

VESTITA PACTA
Agreements clothed with a consideration, as opposed to *nuda pacta,* naked or bare agreements.

VETO
I forbid. A prohibition or the right of forbidding.

VIA
Way. The right to use a way for any purpose.

VIA MEDIA
A middle course.

VICE
In the place of.

VICENA
Near; neighboring.

VIRTUTE OFFICU
By virtue of his office.

VIS
Force; violence.

VOIR DERE
To tell the truth. An examination by the judge or a witness or dependant that is not part of the trial. In the case of a witness this can mean a disqualification.

W

WARRANTIA
A warranty.

MAXIMS

A

ACTA EXTERIORA INDICANT INTERIORA SECRETA
External acts indicate undisclosed thoughts. Exterior acts indicate the intention.

ACTIO PERSONALIS MORITUR CUM PERSONA
A personal right of action dies with the person.

ACTUS CURIAE (OR LEGIS) NEMINEM GRAVABIT
An act of the Court shall prejudice no man. An act of the Court shall hurt no man.

ACTUS DEI NEMINEM GRAVABIT (OR NEMINI NOCET)
An act of God prejudices no man. The Law holds no man responsible for the act of God.

ACTUS NON FACIT REUM, NISI MENS SIT REA
The act itself does not make a man guilty, unless his intention were so. The intent and the act must both concur to constitute the crime.

AD QUAESTIONES FACTI NON RESPONDENT JUDICES; AD QUAESTIONES LEGIS NON RESPONDENT JURATORES
Judges do not answer questions of fact; juries do not answer questions of law.

AFFIRMANTI, NON NEGANTI, INCUMBIT PROBATIO
The burden of proof rests with him who affirms, and not with him who denies a fact.

ALIQUIS NON DEBET ESE JUDEX IN PROPRIA CAUSA, QUIA NON POTEST ESSE JUDEX ET PARS
A man ought not to be a judge in his own cause, for he cannot be at once a judge and a party.

ALLEGANS CONTRARIA NON EST AUDIENDUS
He is not to be heard who alleges things contradictary to each other.

ALLEGANS SUAM TURPITUDINEM NON EST AUDIENDUS

He is not to be heard who alleges his own turpitude or infamy.

AMBIGUITAS VERBORUM LATENS VERIFACTIONE SUPPLETUR; NAM QUOD EX FACTO ORITUR AMBIGUUM VERIFACTIONE FACTI TOLLITUR

Latent or hidden ambiguity of the words may be supplied by evidence; for whatever ambiguity arises from an extrinsic fact, may be removed by extrinsic evidence.

AMBIGUITAS VERBORUM PATENS NULLA VERIFACTIONE EXCLUDITUR

A patent ambiguity cannot be cleared up by extrinsic evidence.

AQUA CEDIT SOLO

Water passes with the soil.

ARGUMENTUM AB INCONVENIENTI EST VALIDUM IN LEGE; QUIA LEX NON PERMITTIT ALIQUOD INCONVENIENS

An argument from that which is inconvenient is good in Law; because the Law will not permit an inconvenience.

ARGUMENTUM AB INCONVENIENTI PLURIMUM VALET IN LEGE

An argument drawn from inconvenience is forcible in Law.

ASSIGNATUS UTITUR JURE AUCTORIS

The assignee makes use of the right of his assignor. An assignee is clothes with the rights of his principal.

AUDI ALTERAM PARTEM

Hear the other side; i.e. no one should be condemned unheard.

A VERBIS LEGIS NON EST RECENDUM

From the words of the law there should be no departure.

B

**BONI JUDICIS EST AMPLIARE JUSTITIAM
(or JURISDICTIONEM)**
> It is the duty of a good judge to extend the limits of
> his justice or jurisdiction.

C

CAVEAT EMPTOR
> That the purchaser take heed.

**CAVEAT EMPTOR; QUI IGNORARE NON DEBUIT
QUOD JUS ALIENUM EMIT**
> Let a purchaser beware; who ought not to be
> ignorant that he is purchasing the rights of another.

CERTUM EST QUOD CERTUM REDDI POTEST
> That is certain which can be rendered certain.

CESSANTE RATIONE LEGIS, CESSAT ET IPSA LEX
> The reason of the law ceases, the law itself ceases.

CONSENSUS TOLLIT ERROREM
> The aquiescence of a party in an error obviates its
> effect.

**CUICUNQUE ALIQUIS QUID CONCEDIT,
CONCEDERE VIDETUR ET ID, SINE QUO RES
IPSA ESSE NON POTUIT (or PERCIPI NON DEBET**
> Whoever grants a thing to any person is supposed
> tacitly to grant that also without which the grant
> itself would be of no effect.

CUJUS EST DARE EST DISPONERE
> Whose it is to give, his it is to dispose.

**CUJUS SOLUM, EJUS EST USQUE AD CELUM
ET AD INFEROS**
> Whoever is the owner of the soil, it is his even to the
> firmament, and to the middle of the earth. Under
> the former would be included buildings; under the
> latter, minerals.

D

DE FIDE ET OFFICIO JUDICIS NON RECIPITUR QUESTION; SED DE SCIENTA SIVE SIT ERROR JURIS SIVE FACTI

The good faith and honesty of a judge cannot be questioned; but otherwise concerning his knowledge, whether he be mistaken as to the law or as to the fact, i.e. his decision may be impugned for error either of law or of fact.

DELAGATA POTESTAS NON POTES DELEGARI

A delegated power cannot be delegated.

DE MINIMUM NON CURAT LEX

The law pays no regard to trifling matters.

DE NON APPARENTIBUS, ET NON EXISTENTIBUS, EADEM EST RATION

As to things not apparent, and those not existing, the rule is the same.

DERIVATIVA PETESTAS NON POTES ESSE MAJOR PRIMITIVA

The derivative power cannot be greater than the primitive. Derived power cannot be greater than that from which it is derived.

DISCRETIO EST SCIRE (or DISCERNERI) PER LEGEM QUID SIT JUSTUM

Discretion is to know through the law what is just.

DOMUS SUA CUIQUE EST TUTISSIMUM REFUGIUM

To every one his own house is the safest refuge. Every man's house is his castle.

DONA CLADESTINA SUNT SEMPER SUSPICIOSA

Clandestine gifts are always suspicious.

E

EQUITYS AGIT IN PERSONAM

Equity acts in person. Equity acts on the person. Equity operates upon the conscience.

EQUITAS EST QUASI EQUALITAS
Equity, is, as it were, equality.

EQUITAS FACTUM HABET QUOD FIERI OPORTUIT
Equity considers that to have been done which ought to have been done.

EQUITAS SEQUITUR LEGEM
Equity follows the law.

EX ANTECEDENTIBUS ET CONSEQUENTIBUS FIT OPTIMA INTERPRETATIO
A passage will be best interpreted by reference to that which precedes and follows it. The best interpretation is made from the context. The context is to be considered in interpreting any phrase or clause, and not the mere isolated phrase or clause.

EX DOLO MALO NON ORITUR ACTIO
A right of action cannot arise out of fraud.

EXECUTIO JURIS NON HABET INJURIAM
The execution of law does no injury.

EXEMPLA ILLUSTRANT, NON RESTRINGUNT LEGEM
Examples illustrate, not restrain, the law.

EX NUDO PACTO NON ORITUR ACTIO
An action does not arise from a bare promise or agreement.

EXPRESSION EORUM QUAE TACITE INSUNT NIHIL OPERATUR
The expressing of those things which are silently implied, has no effect.

EXPRESSION UNIUS EST EXCLUSIO ALTERIUS
The mention of one is the exclusion of another.

EXTRA TERRITORIUM JUS DICENTI IMPUNE NON PARETUR
The sentence of one adjudicating beyond his territory cannot be obeyed with impunity. One may safely disregard a judge administering justice beyond his own country.

F

FALSA DEMONSTRATIO NON NOCET CUM DE CORPORE (or persona) CONSTAT

Mere false description does not vitiate if there be sufficient certainty as to the object, or the person.

FRACTIONEM DIEI NON RECIPIT LEX

The law does not regard the fraction of a day. When, therefore, a thing is to be done upon a particular day, all that day is allowed to do it in.

H

HOMO POTEST ESSE HABILIS ET INHABILIS DIVERSIS TEMPORIBUS

A man may be capable and incapable at different times.

HONESTUM NON EST SEMPER QUOD LICET

That is not always honorable which is lawful, or which the law allows.

HONORIS CAUSA

For the sake of honor.

I

IGNORANTIA FACTI EXCUSAT; IGNORANTIA JURIS (or LEGIS) NON EXCUSAT

Ignorance of fact excuses; ignorance of law does not excuse.

IN AMBIGUA VOCE LEGIS EA POTIUS ACCIPIENDA EST SIGNIFICATIO QUE CARET, PRESERTIM CUM ETIAM VOLUNTAS LEGIS EX HOC COLLIGI POSSIT

In an ambiguous expression of law, that interpretation should be preferred which is most constant with equity, especially where the spirit of the law can be collected from that.

IN ARBITRIM JUDICIS
At the pleasure or discretion of the judge.

IN ARTICULO MORTIS
At the point of death; in a dying state.

IN BANCO
In bench. A judge sitting in banco, in Court, not in chambers.

IN CAMERA
In private; in chambers.

IN CLARIS NON EST LOCUS CONJECTURIS
In things obvious there is no room for conjecture.

INCLUSIO UNIUS EST EXCLUSIO ALTERIUS
The inclusion of one is the exclusion of the other.

INCOMMODUM NON SOLVIT ARGUMENTUS
An inconvenience does not destroy an argument.

IN CONTRACTIBUS TACITE INSUNT QUE SUNT MORIS ET CONSUETUDINIS
Things which are warranted by manner and custom, may be tacitly imported into contracts.

IN CONTRACTIBUS VENIUNT EA QUE SUNT MORIS ET CONSUETUDINIS IN REGIONE IN QUA CONTRAHITUR
In contracts those things occur, which are of law and custom in the place in which the contract is made.

IN CONVENTIONIBUS CONTRAHENTIUM VOLUNTAS PTIUS QUAM VERBA SPECTARI PLACUIT
In contracts the intention of the parties rather than the words actually used by them, should be considered. It must, however, be remembered that in most cases the intention can only be gathered from the words.

IN CRIMINALIBUS PROBATIONES DEBENT ESSE LUCE CLARIORES
In criminal cases, the proofs ought to be clearer than light.

IN CRIMINALIBUS VOLUNTAS PRO FACTO NON REPUTABITUR

In criminal cases, the will will not be taken for the deed.

INDE DATE LEGES NE FORTIOR OMNIA POSSET

The laws are made lest the stronger should be altogether uncontrolled.

IN EMBRYO

In the womb. The business is in an unfinished state, is in its infancy.

IN EQUALI JURE MELIOR EST CONDITIO POSSIDENTIS

Where the right is equal, the condition of the party in actual possession shall prevail. Thus, also, when equities are equal, the law shall prevail.

IN FACTO ET JURE

In fact and in law.

IN FACTO QUOD FINITIUM ET CERTUM EST, NULLUS EST CONJECTURE LOCUS

There is no room for conjecture where the fact is definite and ascertained.

IN FAVOREM VITAE, LIBERTATIS, ET INNOCIENTIAE OMNIA PRAESUMUNTUR

Everything will be presumed in favor of life, liberty and innocence.

IN JURE, NON REMOTA CAUSA, SED PROXIMA SPECTATUR

In law, the immediate and not the remote cause of any event is regarded.

INJURIA NON EXCUSAT INJURIAM

One injury does not excuse or justify another (except in self-defense).

INJURIA PROPRIA NON CADET IN BENEFICIUM FACIENTIS

No one shall profit by (or take advantage of) his own wrong.

IN LOCA PARENTIS

In place of a parent.

IN MALEFICIIS VLUNTAS SPECTATUR NON EXITUS

In criminal acts, the intent is to be taken into consideration and not the result.

IN MALEFICIO RATIHABITIO MANDATO EQUIPARATUR

In offences against the law, a ratification is equal to a command.

IN NOVO CASU, NOVUM REMEDIUM APPONENDDUM EST

A new remedy is to be applied to a new case.

IN OMNIBUS FERE MINORI ETATI SUCCIRRITUR

In nearly all respects a person under age is protected by the law.

IN PERSONAM

To the person; against the person.

IN REM

To or against the property; to the point.

INTER ALIA

Among other things.

INTER PARES NON EST POTESTAS

Among equals, one has not authority over the other.

INTERPRETATIO FACIENDA EST UT RES MAGIS VALEAT QUAM PAREAT

Such an interpretation is to be adopted, that the thing may stand rather than fall.

IN TRANSITU

During the pasage; while in transit.

INTRA VIRES

Within its powers or jurisdiction.

IPSO FACTO

By the very fact itself.

IPSO FACTO AB INITIO

By the deed itself, from (or at) the beginning.

J

JUDEX BONUS NIHIL EX ARBITRIO SUO FACIAT, NEC PROPOSITIONE DOMESTICAE VOLUNTATIS, SED JUXTA LEGES ET JURA PRONUNCIET

A good judge may do nothing from his own judgement, or from a dictate of private will; but he will pronounce according to law and justice.

JURA NATURAE SUNT IMMUTABILIA

The laws of nature are immutable or unchangeable.

JUS CONSTITUI OPORTET IN HIS QUAE UT PLURIMUM ACCIDUNT NON QUAE EX INOPINATO

Law ought to be made with a view to those cases which happen most frequently, and not to those which are of rare or accidental occurrence.

JUS DOMICILII

The law of the domicile.

JUS ET FRAUS NUNQUAM COHABITANT

The law and fraud never live together.

JUS EX INJURIA NON ORITUR

A right cannot arise to anyone out of his own wrong.

JUS PUBLICUM PRIVATORUM PACTIS MUTARI NON POTEST

A public right cannot be altered by private parties.

JUS RESPICIT EQUITATEM

The law pays regard to equity.

JUSTITA NON EST NEGANDA, NON DIFFERENDA

Justice is neither to be denied nor delayed.

L

LATA CULPA DOLO EQUIPARATUR

A gross negligence is tantamount to fraud. Every man is taken to intend that which is the natural consequence of his actions.

LEGES NON VERBIS SED REBUS SUCH IMPOSITAE
Laws are imposed not on words, but on things.

LEGES POSTERIORES PRIORES CONTRARIAS ABROGANT
Subsequent laws repeal prior contrary laws. Later laws repeal earlier laws inconsistent therewith.

LEGIS INTERPRETATION LEGIS VIM OBTINET
The interpretation of law obtains the force of law.

LE SALUT DU PEUPLE EST LA SUPREME LOI
The safety of the people is the highest law.

LES LOIS NE SE CHARGENT DE PUNIR QUE LES ACTIONS EXTERIEURS
Laws change themselves with punishing overt acts only.

LEX DELATIONES SEMPER EXHORRET
The law always abhores delays.

LEX NON COGIT AD IMPOSSIBILIA
The law forces not to impossibilities. The law does not compel a man to do that which he cannot possibly perform.

LEX NON CURAT DE MINIMUS
The law care not about trifles.

LEX SEMPER INTENDIT QUOD CONVENIT RATIONE
The law always intends what is agreeable to reason.

LIBERTAS EST POTESTAS FACIENDI ID QUOD JURE LICET
Liberty is the power of doing that which the law permits.

LIBERTAS EST RES INESTIMABILIS
Liberty is an inestimable thing.

LOU LE LEY CHOSE, LA CEO DONE REMEDIE A VENER A CEO
Where the law gives a right, it gives a remedy to recover.

LUBRICUM LINGUAE NON FACILE TRAHENDUM EST IN POENAM

A slip of the tongue ought not lightly be subjected to punishment.

M

MAGIS DE BONO QUAM DE MALO LEX INTENDIT

The law favors a good rather than a bad construction. Where the words used in a document are susceptible of two meanings, the one in accordance with the law, and the other not so, the former should be adopted.

MAJORI INEST MINUS

The less is contained in the greater.

MAJUS DIGNUM SEIPSUM OCCIDERE QUAM ALIUM

The more worthy draws to itself the less worthy.

MALEFICIA PROPOSITIS DISTINGUUNTUR

Evil deeds are to be distinguished from evil purposes.

MALO ANIMO

With an evil intent.

MALUM NON PRAESUMITUR

Evil is not to be presumed.

MALUS IN UNO MALUS IN OMNIBUS

Bad in one respect, bad in all.

MANIFESTA PROBATIONE NON INDIGENT

Things manifest do not stand in need of proof.

MATTER IN LEY NE SERRA MISE IN BOUTCHE DEL JURORS

Matter of law should not be put into the mouth of jurors.

MAXIMA ILLECEBRA EST PECCANDI IMPUNITATIS SPES

The greatest incitement to wrongdoing is the hope of impunity.

MELIOR EST CONDITIO POSSIDENTIS UBI NEUTER JUS HABIT
Where neither has a right, the condition of the possessor is the better.

MELIOR EST JUSTITIA VERE PRAEVENIENS, QUAM SEVERE PUNIENS
Justice truly preventing is better than severely punishing.

MELIUS EST OMNIA MALA PATI QUAM MALO CONSENTIRE
It is better to suffer every ill than to consent to ill.

MINATUR INNOCENTIBUS QUI PARCIT NOCENTIBUS
He threatens the innocent who spares the guilty.

MISERA EST SERVITUS UBI JUS EST VAGUM AUT INCOGNITUM (or INCERUM)
The slavery is wretched where the law is vague or unknown (or uncertain).

MITIUS IMPERANTI METIUS PARETUR
He is better obeyed who commands leniently.

MODUS ET CONVENTIO VINCUNT LEGEM
The form of agreement and the convention of the parties overrule the law.

MONOPOLIA DICTUR, CUM UNUS SOLUS ALIQUOD GENUS MERCATUREA EMIT PRETIUM AD SUUM LIBITUM STATUENS
It is said to be monopoly when one person alone buys up the whole of one kind of commodity, fixing a price at his own pleasure.

MORA DEBITORIS NON DEBET ESSE CREDITORI DAMNOSA
The delay of the debtor should not go to the damage of the creditor.

MORA REPROBATUR IN LEGE
Delay is reproved in law.

MORS OMNIA SOLVIT
Death dissolves all things.

MORTIS CAUSA
   In prospect of death.

MULTA IN JURE COMMUNI CONTRA RATIONEM DISPUTANDI, PRO COMMUNI UTILITATE, INTRODUCTA SUNT
   Many things contrary to the rule of argument (*i.e.* inconsistent with sound reason) are introduced into the Common Law for common utility.

MULTA NON VETAT LEX, QUAE TAMEN TACITE DAMNAVIT
   The law forbids not many things, which yet it has silently condemned.

MULTI MULTA NEMO OMNIA NOVIT
   Many men know many things; no one knows everything.

MULTIDINEM DECEM FACIUNT
   Ten make a multitude.

MULTITUDO ERRANTIUM NON PARIT ERRORI PATROCINIUM
   The multitude of those who err gives no excuse to the error.

N

NAM QUE HAERET IN LITERA HAERET IN CORTICE
   He who considers merely the letter of an instrument, goes but skin-deep into its meaning.

NATURA APPETIT PERFECTUM ITA ET LEX
   Nature desires perfection; so also law.

NATURA NON FACIT SALTUM; ITA NEX LEX
   Nature takes no leap; so neither does law.

NECESSARIUM EST QUOD NON POTEST ALITER SE HABERE
That which is necessary cannot be otherwise.

NECESSITAS EST LEX TEMPORIS ET LOCI
Necessity is the law of time and place.

NECESSITAS NON HABET LEGEM
Necessity has no law.

NEGLIGENTA SEMPER HABIT INFORTUNIUM COMITEM
Negligence always has misfortune for a companion.

NEMINEM OPORTET ESSE SAPIENTOREM LEGIBUS
No man, out of his private reason ought to be wiser than the laws.

NEMO AGIT IN SEIPSUM
No one acts against himself.

NEMO ALLEGANS, SUAM TURPITUDINEM AUDIENDUS EST
No one alleging his own baseness ought to be heard.

NEMO BIS PUNITUR AUT VEXATUR PRO DELICTO
No one is to be twice punished or vexed for the same fault or offense.

NEMO DAMNUM FACIT NISI ID FACIT QUOD FACERE JUS NON HABET
No one is a wrong-doer, but he who does what the law does not allow.

NEMO DAT QUI NON HABET
He who has not, cannot give.

NEMO DEBET ESSE JUDEX IN PROPRIA CAUSA
No one can be a judge in his own cause.

NEMO DEBET EX ALIENA JACTURA LUCRARI
No person ought to gain by another person's loss.

NEMO EX DOLO SUO PROPRIO RELEVETUR, AUT AUXILIUM CAPIAT
Let no one be relieved or gain an advantage by his own fraud.

NEMO MORITURUS PRAESUMITUR MENTIRE
No one about to die is presumed to lie.

NEMO PLUS JURIS IN ALIUM TRANSFERRE POTEST, QUAM IPSE HABET
No man can transfer to another a right or title greater than he himself possesses.

NEMO POTEST FACERE PER ALIUM, QUOD PER SE NON POTEST
No one can do through another what he cannot do through himself.

NEMO PRAESUMITUR MALUS
No one is presumed to be bad.

NEMO TEUTUR AD IMPOSSIBILE
No one is bound to an impossibility.

NEMO TENETUR DIVINARE
No one is bound to foretell.

NEMO TENETUR PRODERE SELPSUM
No one is bound to betray himself. No one can be compelled to criminate himself.

NIENT CULPABLE
Not guilty.

NIHIL DEBET FORUM EX SCENA
The Court has nothing to do with what is not before it.

NIHIL FACIT ERROR NOMINIS CUM DE CORPORE CONSTATE
An error as to a name is nothing when there is certainty as to the person.

NIHIL IS LEGE INTOLERABILIUS EST, EANDEM REM DIVERSO JURE CENSERI
Nothing in law is more intolerable than to rule a similar case by a diverse law.

NIHIL MAJIS JUSTUM EST QUAM QUOD NECESSARIUM EST
Nothing is more just than what is necessary.

NIHIL PERFECTUM EST DUM ALIQUID RESTAT AGENDUM

Nothing is perfect while anything remains to be done.

NIHIL QUOD EST CONTRA RATIONEM EST LICITUM

Nothing is permitted which is contrary to reason.

NIHIL SIMUL INVENTUM EST ET PERFECTUM

Nothing is invented and perfected at the same moment.

NIHIL TAM PROPRIUM EST IMPERII QUAM LEGIBUS VIVERE

Nothing is so much the property of sovereignty as to live according to the laws.

NIL CONSENSUI TAM CONTRARIUM EST QUAM VIS ATQUE METUS

There is nothing so opposed to consent as force and fear (coercion and threat).

NOMEN NON SUFFICIT SI RES NON SIT DE JURE AUT DE FACTO

The name is not sufficient if the thing be not by law or by fact.

NON CAPITUR QUI JUS PUBLICUM SEQUITUR

To insist upon a rule of public law is not to over-reach.

NON CULPA NISI MEN SIT REA

There is no guilt unless there be a guilty intention.

NON DECIPTIUR QUI SCIT SE DECIPI

He is not deceived who knows himself to be deceived.

NON EST REGULA QUIN FALLAT

There is no rule which may not fail.

NON FACIAS MALUM, UT INDE VENIAT BONUM

You are not to do evil so that good may come from it.

NON JURE FACTUM

Not made by law.

NON OMNE QUOD LICET HONESTUM EST
Not everything which the law allows is honorable. A person may keep within the strict letter of the law and even within the strict rules of equity, so as not to be liable either at law or in equity, and yet his conduct under the circumstances may not be honorable, but morally detestable.

NON PERTINENT AD JUDICEM SECULAREM COGNOSCERE DE IIS QUAE SUNT MERE SPIRITUALIA ANNEXA
It belongs not to the secular judge to take cognizance of things which are merely spiritual.

NON QUOD DICTUM SED QUOD FACTUM INSPICIENDUM EST
Not what is said but what is done is to be looked to. Equity looks to the intent rather than to the form, for equity would in no case permit the veil of form to hide the true effect or intention of the transaction.

NON REFERT QUID NOTUM SIT JUDICI, SI-NETUM NON SIT IN FORMA JUDICI
It matters not what is known to the judge, if it is not known in judicial form, *i.e.,* if he has not judicial cognizance of it.

NON SOLENT QUAE ABUNDANT VITIARE SCRIPTURAS
Surplusage or irrelevant matter do not vitiate a written instrument.

NON TEMERE CREDERE EST NERVUS SAPIENTIAE
Not to believe rashly is the nerve of wisdom.

NON VIDENTUR QUI ERRANT CONSENTIRE
They are not supposed to consent who commit a mistake. They are not considered to consent who act under a mistake.

NOSCITUR A SOCIIS
He is known by his companions.

NOVA CONSTITUTIO FUTURIS FORMAM IMPONERE DEBET, NON PRAETERITIS

A new law ought to impose form on what is to follow, not on the past. New legislation ought to be prospective not retrospective in its operation.

NOXA CAPUT SEQUITUR

Guilt follows the principal.

NUDUM PACTUM EX QUO NON ORITUR ACTIO

A naked or base agreement out of which no cause action arises.

NULLA INTELLIGITUR MORA IBI FIERI UBI NULLA PETITIO EST

No delay of payment is meant to have been made when there has been no demand.

NULLUM INIQUUEM EST PROESUMENDUM IN JURE

No inequity is presumed in the law.

NULLUS COMMODUM CAPERE POTEST DE INJURIA SUA PROPRIA

No one can take advantage of his own wrong.

NULLUS DICITUR ACCESSORIUS POST FELONIAM, SED ILLE QUI NOVIT PRINCIPALEM FELONIAM FECISSE, ET ILLUM RECEPTAVIT ET COMFORTAVIT

No one is called an accessory after the fact but he who knew the principal to have committed a felony, and received and comforted him.

NUNQUAM CRESCIT EX POST FACTO PRAETERITI DELICTI AESTIMATIO

The estimation of a past offense is never increased by an after fact. A later fact will not be allowed to extend or amplify a past offense.

NUNQUAM NIMIS DICITUR QUOD NUNQUAM SATIS DICITUR

What is never sufficiently said is never said too much.

O

OBEDIENTIA EST LEGIS ESSENTIA
Obedience is the essence of law.

OBLIGATIO MANDATI CONSENSU CONTRAHENTIUM CONSISTIT
The authority of an agent to contract for his principal rests on the consent of his principal.

OBTEMPERANDUM EST CONSUETUDINI RATIONABILI TANQUAM LEGI
A reasonable custom is to be obeyed like law.

OMNES LICENTIAM HABERE HIS, QUAE PRO SE INTRODUCTA SUNT RENUNCIARE
Every man may renounce a benefit which the law has conferred upon him.

OMNIA PRAESUMUNTUR CONTRA SPOLIATOREM
All things are presumed against a wrong-doer.

OMNIA PRAESUMUNTUR RITE ET SOLENNITER ESSE ACTA DONEC PROBETUR IN CONTRARIUM
All things are presumed to have been rightly and duly performed until the contrary is proved.

OPTIMA EST LEGIS INTERPRES CONSUETUDO
Custom is the best interpreter of the laws.

OPTIMA EST LEX QUAE MINUMUM RELINQUIT ARBITRIO JUDICIS: OPTIMUS JUDEX QUI MINIMUM SIBI
That system of law is best which confides as little as possible to the discretion of the judge; that judge the best who relies as little as possible on his own opinion.

P

PACTA DANT LEGEM CONTRACTUI
The stipulations of parties constitute the law of the contract.

PARIA COPULANTUR PARIBUS

Like things unite with like. Birds of a feather flock together.

PAR IN PAREM IMPERIUM NON HABET

An equal has no power over an equal.

PARUM PROFICIT SCIRE QUID FIERI DEBET, SI NON COGNOSCAS QUOMODO SIT FACTURUM

It avails little to know what ought to be done, if you do not know how it is done.

PENDENTE LITE NIHIL INNOVETUR

During a litigation nothing new should be introduced.

PERICULUM REI VENDITAE, NONDUM TRADITAE, EST EMPTORIS

The risk of a thing sold, and not yet delivered, is the purchaser's.

PLUS PECCAT AUCTOR QUAM ACTOR

The causer offends more than the performer.

PLUS VALET QUOD AGITUR QUAM QUOD SIMULATE CONCIPITUR

What is done avails more than what is pretended to be done.

PLUS VALET UNUS OCULATUS TESTIS QUAM AURITI DECEM

One eye-witness is better than ten ear-witnesses.

POENA AD MENSURAM DELICIT STATUENDA EST

Punishment is to be measured by the extent of the offense.

POSSESSIO EST QUASI PEDIS POSITIO

Possession, is, as it were, the position of the foot. Possession is nine-tenths of the law.

PRIVILEGIUM NON VALET CONTRA REM PUBLICAM

A privilege avails not against public good or against the interests of the public.

PRUDENTER AGIT QUI PRAECEPTO LEGIS OBTEMPERAT

He acts prudently, who obeys the command of the law.

Q

QUAE AB INITIO INUTILIS FUIT INSTITUTIO EX POST FACTO VCONVALESCERE NON POTEST

That which was a useless instutution at the commencement cannot grow strong by an after-fact.

QUAE DUBITATIONIS CAUSA TOLLENDAE INSERUNTUR COMMUNEM LEGEM NON LAUDUNT

Things which are inserted for the purpose of removing doubt, hurt not the common law.

QUAAE COMMUNI LEGI DEROGANT STRICTE INTERPRETENTUR

Things which are derogate from the common law are to be strictly interpreted.

QUAE CONTRA RETIONEM JURIS INTRODUCTA SUNT, NON DEBENT TRAHI IN CONSEQUENTIAM

Things introduced contrary to the reason of law, ought not to be drawn into a precedent.

QUAECUNQUE INTRA RATIONEM LEGIS INVENTUNTUR INTRA LEGEM IPSAM ESSE JUDICANTUR

What things so ever appear within the reason of law are to be considered within the law itself.

QUAE DUBITATIONIS CAUSA TOLLENDAE INSERUNTUR, JUS COMMUNE NON LAEDUNT

Clauses inserted in contracts to take away all ground for doubt, hurt not the common law.

QAUE IN TESTAMENTO ITA SUNT SCRIPTA UT INTELLIGE NON POSSINT, PRINDE SUNT AC SI SCRIPTA NON ESSENT

What has been so written in a will as to be unintelligible, is to be regarded as though it had not been written.

QUAELIBET POENA CORPORALIS, QUAMVIS MINIMA, MAJOR EST QUALIBET POENA PECUNIARIA

Every corporeal punishment, although the very least, is greater than any pecuniary punishment.

QUAE MALA SUNT INCHOATA IN PRINCIPIO VIX BONA PERAGUNTUR EXITU

Things bad in principle at the commencement seldom achieve a good end.

QUAERERE DAT SAPERE QUAE SUNT LEGITIMA VERE

To inquire into is the way to know what things are lawful.

QUANDO ALIQUID PROHIBETUR, PROHIBETUR OMNE PER QUOD DEVENITUR AD ILLUD

When anything is prohibited, everything which tends towards it is also prohibited.

QUANDO LEX ALIQUID ALICUI CONCEDIT, CONCEDERE VIDETUR ID SINE QUO RES IPSA ESSE NON POTEST

When the law gives a man anything, it gives him that without which it cannot exist.

QUI ACCUSAT INTEGRAE SIT ET NON CRIMINOSUS

Let him who accuses be of clear fame and not criminal.

QUI ALIQUID STATUERIT PARTE INAUDITA ALTERA, AEQUUM LICET DEXERIT, HAUD AEQUUM FACERIT

He who decides anything, one party being unheard, though he should decide right, does wrong.

QUICUD EST CONTRA NORMAN RECTI, EST INJURIA

Whatever is against the rule of right, is an injury.

QUICUD IN EXCESSU ACTUM EST LEGE PROHIBETUR

Whatever is done in excess is prohibited in law.

135

QUICUD PLANTATUR (or FIXATUR or INAEDIFICATUR) SOLO, SOLO CEDIT

Whatever is fixed to the soil, goes with or belongs to the soil.

QUI FACIT PER ALLU, FACIT (or EST PERINDE AC SI FACIAT) PER SE

He who acts through another (is in the same position as if he) acts through himself.

QUI JURE SUO UTITUR, NEMINEM LOEDIT (or NEMINI FACIT INJURIAM)

He who exercises his right does an injustice to nobody.

QUI PARCIT NOCENTIBUS, INNOCENTIBUS PUNIT

He who spares the guilty, punishes the innocent.

QUI PER FRAUDEM AGIT, FRUSTA AGIT

What a man does fraudently, he does in vain.

QUI PRIOR EST TEMPORE, POTIOR EST JURE

He who is first in point of time is more powerful in law.

QUI SENTIT COMMODUM SENTIRE DEBET ET ONUS; ET E CONTRA

He who receives the advantage, ought to suffer the burden; and on the contrary.

QUI TACET CONSENTIRE VIDETUR

He who is silent appears to consent.

QUOD FIERI NON DEBET (or DEBUIT) FACTUM VALET

What should not be done, yet being done, shall be valid.

QUOD VANUM ET INUTILE EST, LEX NON REQUIRIT

The law requires not what is vain and useless.

QUOTIES IN VERBIS NULLA EST AMBIGUTAS, IBI NULLA EXPOSITIO CONTRA VERBA FIENDA EST

When in the words there is no ambiguity, no

136

exposition shall be made which is opposed to the express words of the instrument, *i.e.,* parol evidence to contradict or vary the clear words of a written instrument is inadmissible.

R

RATIO ET AUCTORITAS DUO CLARISSIMA MUNDI LUMINA

Reason and authority are the two brightest lights of the world.

RECEDITUR A PLACITIS JURIS POTIUS QUAM INJURIAE ET DELICTA MANEANT IMPUNITA

We surrender the forms of law rather than allow injuries to remain unpunished.

RECURRENDUM ESTAD EXTRAORDINARIUM QUANDO NON VALET ORDINARIUM

We must have recourse to what is extraordinary, when what is ordinary fails.

REGULA EX JURE, NON JUS EX REGULA SUMITUR

The practice is taken from the law not the law from the practice.

REMISSIUS IMPERANTI MELIUS PARETUR

A man commanding not too strictly is better obeyed.

RES INTER ALIOS ACTA ALTERI NOCERE NON DEBET

Things done between strangers ought not to injure a party. A matter litigated between two parties ought not to prejudice a third party.

REX DATUR PROPTER REGNUM, NON REGNUM PROPTER REGEM

A king is given to serve the kingdom, not the kingdom to serve the king.

S

SALUS POPULI EST SUPREME LEX

The safety of the people is the supreme law.

137

SAPIENTA LEGIS NUMMARIO PRETIO NON EST AESTIMANDA

The wisdom of the law cannot be measured by money.

SAPIENS OMNI AGIT CUM CONCILIO

A wise man does everything advisedly.

SAPIENTA SUPPLET AETATEM

Widsom supplies the want of age.

SATIUS EST PETERE FONTES QUAM SECTARI RIVULOS

It is better to seek the sources than to follow the streamlets, *i.e.,* it is better not to trust to quotations.

SEMPER PRAESUMITUR PRO MATRIMONIO

The presumption is always in favor of the validity of a marriage.

SENTENTIA FACIT JUS, ET LEGIS INTERPRETATIO LEGIS VIM OBTINET

Judgment creates the right, and the interpretation of the law has the force of law.

SEQUI DEBET POTENTIA JUSTITIAM, NON PRAECEDERE

Power should follow justice, not precede it.

SERMO EST INDEX ANIMI

Speech is the index of the mind.

SIC UTERI TUO UT ALIENUM NON LAEDAS

Use your own property in such a manner as not to injure that of another. So use your own property as not to injure *the rights* of another.

SUMMUM JUS, SUMMA INJURIA

Extreme law is extreme injury. The strict enforcement of a law sometimes works a great wrong.

T

TANTUM BONA VALENT, QUANTUM VENDI POSSUNT

Things are worth what they will sell for.

TESTIMONIA PONDERANDA SUNT, NON ENUMERANDA

Evidence is to be weighed, not enumerated. No particular number of witnesses should be required for the proof of any fact.

TUTIUS SEMPER EST ERRARE ACQUITANDO QUAM IN PUNIEMDO; EX PARTE MISERICORDIAE QUAM EX PARTE JUSTITIAE

It is always safer to err in acquitting than in punishing; on the side of mercy than of strict justice. Thus arises the presumption of innocence, until conviction.

U

UBI CESAT REMEDIUM ORDINARIUM, IBI DECURRITUR AD EXTRAORDINARIUM, ET NUNQUAM DECURITUR AD EXTRAORDINARIUM UBI VALET ORDINARIUM

Where the ordinary remedy fails, that recourse must be had to an extraordinary one, but recourse is never had to the extraordinary where the ordinary is sufficient.

UBI CUNQUE EST INJURIA IBI DAMNUM SEQUITUR

Where there is an injury, there a loss or damage follows.

UBI JUS, IBI REMEDIUM

Where there is a right, there is always a remedy. Equity will not suffer a wrong to be without remedy.

UBI JUS UNV ERTUM, IBI JUS NULLUM

Where the law is uncertain, there is no law.

UBI NON EST COGENDI AUCTORITAS, IBI NON EST PARENDI NECESSITAS

Where there is no authority to compel, there is no authority to obey.

V

VANA EST ILLA POTENTIA QUAE NUNQUAM VENIT IN ACTUM
Vain is that power which never comes into play.

VERITAS EST JUSTITAE MATER
Truth is the mother of justice.

VIGILANTIBUS, NON DORMIENTIBUS, JURA SUBVENIUNT
Laws come to the assistance of the vigilant, not of the sleepy.

VIOLENTI NON FIT INJURIA
That to which a man consents cannot be considered an injury.

LEGAL ALMANAC SERIES CONVERSION TABLE
List of Original Titles and Authors

1. LAW OF MARRIAGE AND DIVORCE, R.V. MacKay
2. HOW TO MAKE A WILL SIMPLIFIED, P.J.T. Callahan
3. LAW OF ADOPTION, M.L. Leavy
4. LAW OF REAL ESTATE, P.J.T. Callahan
5. IMMIGRATION LAWS OF THE UNITED STATES, C.M. Crosswell
6. GUARDIANSHIP LAW, R.V. MacKay
7. LABOR LAW, C. Rachlin
8. HOW TO BECOME A CITIZEN OF THE U.S., Margaret E. Hall
9. SEX AND THE STATUTORY LAW, Part I, R.V. Sherwin
9a. SEX AND THE STATUTORY LAW, Part II, R.V. Sherwin
10. LAW OF DEBTOR AND CREDITOR, L.G. Greene
11. LANDLORD AND TENANT, F.H. Kuchler
12. LAW OF SUPPORT, F.H. Kuchler
13. CIVIL RIGHTS AND CIVIL LIBERTIES, E.S. Newman
14. LAW OF NOTARIES PUBLIC, L.G. Greene
15. LAW OF LIBEL AND SLANDER, E.C. Thomas
16. LIQUOR LAWS, B.M. Bernard
17. EDUCATION LAW, D.T. Marke
18. LAW OF MISSING PEOPLE, F. Fraenkel
19. STATE WORKMEN'S COMPENSATION, W.R. Dittmar
20. LAW OF MEDICINE, P.J.T. Callahan
21. HOW TO SECURE COPYRIGHT, R. Wincor
22. JUVENILE DELINQUENCY, F.B. Sussman
23. LAWS CONCERNING RELIGION, A. Burstein
24. ELECTION LAWS, B.M. Bernard
25. DRIVER'S MANUAL, T. Mattern & A.J. Mathes
26. STATE SOCIAL SECURITY LAWS, S.H. Asch
27. MANUAL OF CIVIL AVIATION LAW, T. Mattern & A.J. Mathes
28. HOW TO PROTECT AND PATENT YOUR INVENTION, I. Mandell
29. LAW FOR THE SMALL BUSINESSMAN, M.L. Leavy
30. INSANITY LAWS, W.R. Dittmar
31. HOW TO SERVE ON A JURY, P. Francis
32. CRIMES AND PENALTIES, T.B. Stuchiner
33. LAW OF INHERITANCE, E.M. Wypyski
34. HOW TO CHANGE YOUR NAME, L.G. Greene
35. LAW OF ACCIDENTS, W.M. Kunstler
36. LAW OF CONTRACTS, R. Wincor
37. LAW OF INSURANCE, I.M. Taylor
38. LAW OF PHILANTHROPY, E.S. Newman
39. LAW OF SELLING, J.A. Hoehlein
40. LAW OF PERSONAL LIBERTIES, R. Schwartzmann
41. LAW OF BUYING AND SELLING, B.R. White
42. PRACTICAL AND LEGAL MANUAL FOR THE INVESTOR, S.I. Kaufman
43. LAW FOR THE HOMEOWNER, REAL ESTATE OPERATOR, AND BROKER, L.M. Nussbaum
44. LAW FOR THE TOURIST, R.J. DeSeife
45. LAW FOR THE FAMILY MAN, L.F. Jessup
46. LEGAL STATUS OF YOUNG ADULTS, P.J.T. Callahan
47. LAW AND THE SPORTSMAN, R.M. Debevec
48. LAW OF RETIREMENT, L.F. Jessup
49. LAW FOR THE PET OWNER, D.S. Edgar
50. ESTATE PLANNING, P.J. Goldberg
51. TAX PLANNING, P.J. Goldberg
52. LEGAL PROTECTION FOR THE CONSUMER, S. Morganstern
53. LEGAL STATUS OF WOMEN, P. Francis
54. PRIVACY—ITS LEGAL PROTECTION, H. Gross
55. PROTECTION THROUGH THE LAW, P. Francis
56. LAW OF ART AND ANTIQUES, S. Hodes
57. LAW OF DEATH AND DISPOSAL OF THE DEAD, H.Y. Bernard
58. LAW DICTIONARY OF PRACTICAL DEFINITIONS, E.J. Bander
59. LAW OF ENGAGEMENT AND MARRIAGE, F.H. Kuchler
60. CONDEMNATION: YOUR RIGHTS WHEN GOVERNMENT ACQUIRES YOUR PROPERTY, G. Lawrence
61. CONFIDENTIAL AND OTHER PRIVILEGED COMMUNICATION, R.D. Weinberg
62. UNDERSTANDING THE UNIFORM COMMERCIAL CODE, D. Lloyd
63. WHEN AND HOW TO CHOOSE AN ATTORNEY, C.K. Wehringer
64. LAW OF SELF-DEFENSE, F.S. & J. Baum
65. ENVIRONMENT AND THE LAW, I.J. Sloan
66. LEGAL PROTECTION IN GARNISHMENT AND ATTACHMENT, S. Morganstern
67. HOW TO BE A WITNESS, K. Tierney
68. AUTOMOBILE LIABILITY AND THE CHANGING LAW, M.G. Woodroof
69. PENALTIES FOR MISCONDUCT ON THE JOB, A. Avins
70. LEGAL REGULATION OF CONSUMER CREDIT, S. Morganstern
71. RIGHT OF ACCESS TO INFORMATION FROM THE GOVERNMENT, S.D. Thurman
72. COOPERATIVES AND CONDOMINIUMS, P.E. Kehoe
73. RIGHTS OF CONVICTS, H.I. Handman
74. FINDING THE LAW-GUIDE TO LEGAL RESEARCH, D. Lloyd
75. LAWS GOVERNING BANKS AND THEIR CUSTOMERS, S. Mandell
76. HUMAN BODY AND THE LAW, C.L. Levy
77. HOW TO COPE WITH U.S. CUSTOMS, A.I. Demcy

LEGAL ALMANAC SERIES CONVERSION TABLE
List of Present Titles and Authors